Alison Smith

ESSENTIALS

GCSE AQA

Anthology: Conflict

Acknowledgements

The author and publisher are grateful for permission to use quoted materials:

p. 4-5, 42-43, 46, 'Flag' by John Agard from *Half-Caste and Other Poems* (Hodder Children's, 2004), copyright ©John Agard 2004, reprinted by permission of Hodder Children's, an imprint of Hachette Children's Books, 338 Euston Road, London NW1 3BH.

p. 6-7, 46, *'Extract from* Out of the Blue' by Simon Armitage from *Out of the Blue* (Enitharmon Press, 2008), reprinted by permission of Enitharmon Press.

p. 8-9, 36-37, 39, 46, 'Mametz Wood' by Owen Sheers from *Skirrid Hill* (Seren, 2006), reprinted by permission of the author c/o Rogers Coleridge and White, 20 Powis Mews, London W11 1JN.

p. 10-11, 'The Yellow Palm' by Robert Minhinnick from *King Driftwood* (Carcanet, 2008), reprinted by permission of Carcanet Press Ltd.

p. 12-13, 40-41, 46, 'The Right Word' by Imtiaz Dharker from *The Terrorist at my Table* (Bloodaxe Books, 2006), reprinted by permission of Bloodaxe Books.

p. 14-15, 42-43, 46, 'At the Border, 1979' by Choman Hardi from *Life for Us* (Bloodaxe Books, 2004), reprinted by permission of Bloodaxe Books.

p. 16-17, 'Belfast Confetti' by Ciaran Carson (The Gallery Press, 2008). By kind permission of the author and The Gallery Press, Loughcrew, Oldcastle, County Meath, Ireland, from *Collected Poems* (2008).

p. 18-19, 47, 'Poppies' by Jane Weir, published by the *Guardian Review* July 2009, copyright ©Jane Weir 2009, reprinted by permission of Templar Poetry.

p. 24-25, 47, 'Bayonet Charge' by Ted Hughes originally from *Hawk in the Rain* (Faber, 1957), reprinted by permission of the publishers, Faber & Faber Ltd.

p. 26-27, 47, 'The Falling Leaves' by Margaret Postgate Cole found in an anthology *Scars Upon My Heart* collected by Catherine Reilly (Virago, 1981), reprinted by permission of David Higham Associates.

p. 28-29, 47, 'Come On, Come Back' by Stevie Smith, copyright ©Stevie Smith 1975, from *The Collected Poems of Stevie Smith* (New Directions, 1983/Penguin, 1985), reprinted by permission of The Estate of James MacGibbon.

p. 30-31, 47, 'next to of course god america i'. Copyright 1926, 1954, ©1991 by the Trustees for the E.E. Cummings Trust. Copyright ©1985 by George James Firmage, from *Complete Poems 1904-1962* by E.E. Cummings, edited by George J. Firmage. Used by permission of Liveright Publishing Corporation.

p. 32-33, 47, 'Hawk Roosting' by Ted Hughes from *Collected Poems* (Faber, 2003), copyright ©The Estate of Ted Hughes 2003, reprinted by permission of the publishers, Faber & Faber Ltd.

Contents

Poetry Across Time
Revised

The Poetry Exam

Flag

The subject of the poem is only mentioned here and at the very end. The questions throughout the poem are answered by the title.

The impact of the flag is juxtaposed with the flag itself to show the power that we attribute to it.

Question and answer format encourages the reader to consider the questions and answers in detail.

Flag

What's that fluttering in a breeze?
It's just a piece of cloth
that brings a nation to its knees.

What's that unfurling from a pole?
5 It's just a piece of cloth
that makes the guts of men grow bold.

What's that rising over a tent?
It's just a piece of cloth
that dares the coward to relent.

10 What's that flying across a field?
It's just a piece of cloth
that will outlive the blood you bleed.

How can I possess such a cloth?
Just ask for a flag, my friend.
15 Then blind your conscience to the end.

The verbs which describe the movement of the flag are all understated.

Dual meaning: either that people kneel before the flag, or that it is the cause of people begging for mercy.

If you look carefully at the layout of the stanzas, they almost look like flags.

A reminder that people die for their countries.

The turn in the poem marks a change in the tone.

Sums up the poet's feelings about patriotism. It's clearly a very cynical view.

Key Features

Repetition   Verbs   Emotive language

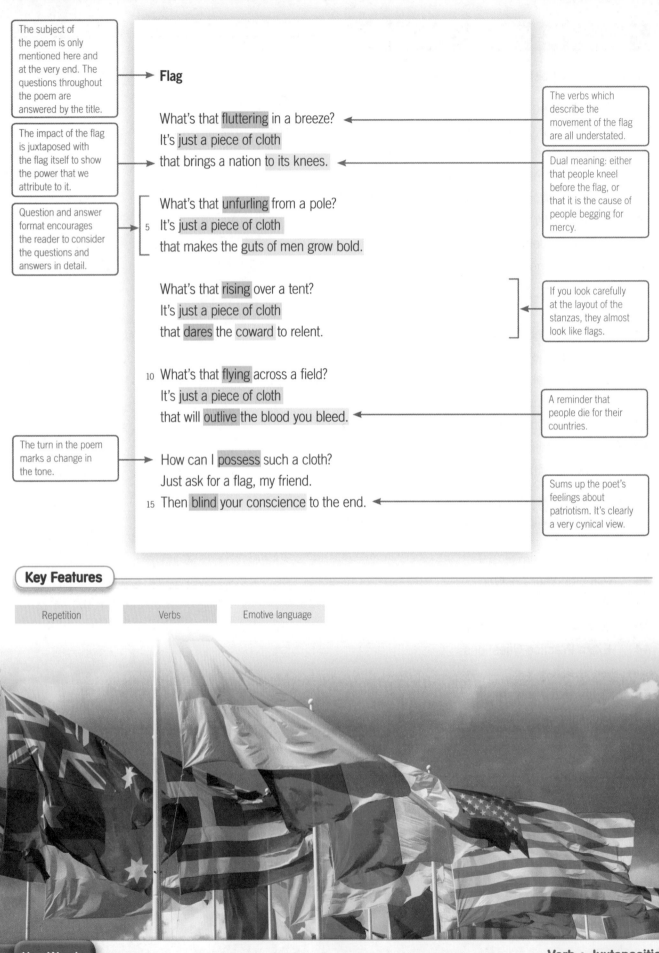

About the Poem

- Written by **John Agard** (1949–).

- Written as a series of questions which consider the significance and symbolism of a flag.

- The questions encourage the reader to think about patriotism and the consequences of being patriotic.

- At the end of the poem, Agard suggests that being patriotic is not the positive thing that it is presented as.

Ideas, Themes and Issues

- **Patriotism**: Flags are a powerful symbol of a country and allegiance to the flag demonstrates patriotism. The poet considers the consequences of patriotism and whether being patriotic is as straightforward as people think.

- **Symbols of conflict**: The flag has a great deal of power of influence because of the way in which people view it. People can use their patriotism as a kind of excuse for conflict.

- **Warning**: The poem is an unusual way of suggesting the danger of conflict.

Form, Structure and Language

- The poem is written in a **question and answer structure** which makes the reader think about the idea of a flag.

- The **verbs** used to describe how the flag moves are understated and calm. The poet **juxtaposes** this with **emotive language** to describe the effect of the flag.

- The verbs are in the **present tense** to suggest that these things are happening now.

- The **dismissive** 'just' helps to show that the flag is something very simple which has been given significance by the way in which people regard it.

- There are lots of examples of **dual meanings** in the poem, such as lines 3 and 6, showing that things are not always clear cut.

- The **layout** of the stanzas on the page, with the shorter middle line, makes the poem look like a succession of flags flying.

- **Repetition** adds emphasis to the last stanza where the pattern of the poem changes.

- The **turn** in the poem at line 13 signals a **change in tone**, as the questioner wants the power of the flag.

- The simple sentence in the last line sums up the poet's **cynical** views about patriotism.

Quick Test

1. What effect does the flag have on people?
2. How does the poet use language to show his feeling about the flag?
3. When the poet says 'my friend' in line 14, do you think he means it?
4. What does the poet think of people who are blindly patriotic?

Extract from Out of the Blue

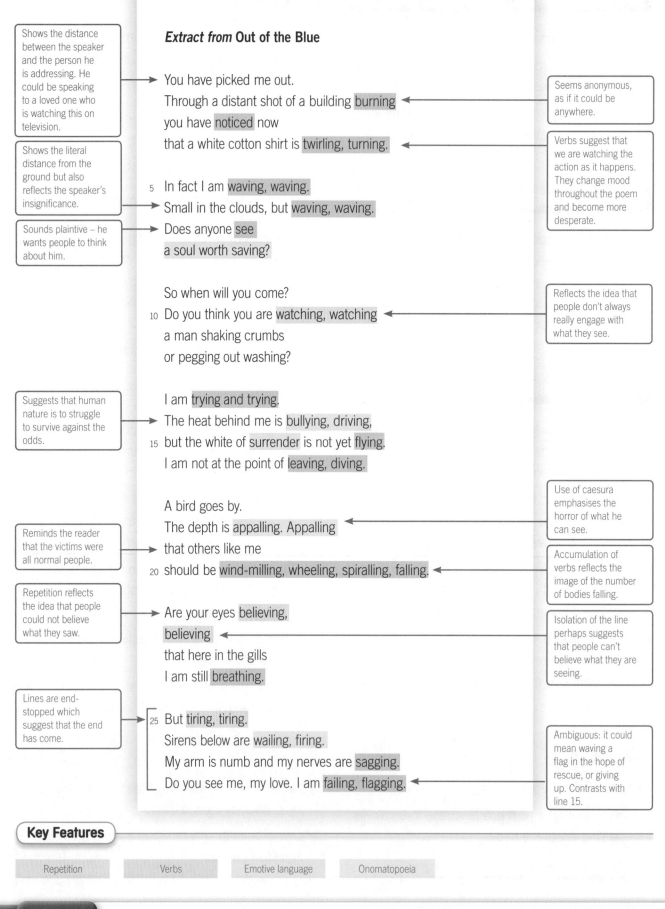

Shows the distance between the speaker and the person he is addressing. He could be speaking to a loved one who is watching this on television.

Shows the literal distance from the ground but also reflects the speaker's insignificance.

Sounds plaintive – he wants people to think about him.

Suggests that human nature is to struggle to survive against the odds.

Reminds the reader that the victims were all normal people.

Repetition reflects the idea that people could not believe what they saw.

Lines are end-stopped which suggest that the end has come.

Extract from Out of the Blue

You have picked me out.
Through a distant shot of a building burning
you have noticed now
that a white cotton shirt is twirling, turning.

5 In fact I am waving, waving.
Small in the clouds, but waving, waving.
Does anyone see
a soul worth saving?

So when will you come?
10 Do you think you are watching, watching
a man shaking crumbs
or pegging out washing?

I am trying and trying.
The heat behind me is bullying, driving,
15 but the white of surrender is not yet flying.
I am not at the point of leaving, diving.

A bird goes by.
The depth is appalling. Appalling
that others like me
20 should be wind-milling, wheeling, spiralling, falling.

Are your eyes believing,
believing
that here in the gills
I am still breathing.

25 But tiring, tiring.
Sirens below are wailing, firing.
My arm is numb and my nerves are sagging.
Do you see me, my love. I am failing, flagging.

Seems anonymous, as if it could be anywhere.

Verbs suggest that we are watching the action as it happens. They change mood throughout the poem and become more desperate.

Reflects the idea that people don't always really engage with what they see.

Use of caesura emphasises the horror of what he can see.

Accumulation of verbs reflects the image of the number of bodies falling.

Isolation of the line perhaps suggests that people can't believe what they are seeing.

Ambiguous: it could mean waving a flag in the hope of rescue, or giving up. Contrasts with line 15.

Key Features

Repetition   Verbs   Emotive language   Onomatopoeia

Extract from Out of the Blue

About the Poem

- Written by **Simon Armitage** (1963–).

- The poem was commissioned to commemorate the terrorist attacks in New York in September 2001. This extract is part of a much longer poem.

- The poem opens with the speaker describing being in one of the World Trade Center buildings after the attack. He is speaking to an unnamed other, who is watching the scene on television.

- To begin with, the speaker seems confident of being rescued.

- As the poem continues, it becomes clear that he will not be saved, and the only outcome will be his death.

Ideas, Themes and Issues

- **Reality of conflict**: The poem vividly describes what it must be like to be caught in the middle of a conflict.

- **Impact on the individual**: The speaker is not really a part of the conflict; he is an innocent bystander.

Form, Structure and Language

- The poem is **elegiac**: it is a mournful commemoration of the dead.

- The poem is written in the **first person** which gives it a sense of immediacy and makes the reader feel that they are watching events as they unfold.

- **Verbs** help to evoke the sense that we are helpless observers. They change throughout the poem to reflect the **changing mood** of the speaker, for example 'twirling', 'waving' and 'diving'.

- The use of **questions** in the poem reflects the confusion and fear of the speaker, but also helps to challenge the readers' perceptions of events.

- The **caesura** in line 18 emphasises the horror of what the speaker can see.

- The language is **colloquial** and this is reflected in the line 'others like me' which shows that the victims were ordinary people.

- The **accumulation** in line 20 emphasises the number of victims as well as their movement as they fell.

- The **onomatopoeia** in line 26 is suggestive of the **sounds** of the sirens but also of the cries of the victims.

- In the final **stanza**, the lines are all **end-stopped**. This gives it an air of finality.

Quick Test

1. How does the poet suggest that the people involved are ordinary people?

2. How does the poet suggest the horror of this event?

3. How does the poet show that this event was something that affected people who weren't even there?

Mametz Wood

Mametz Wood

Opens in the past and reminds us that they are the remains of a long-ago war.

For years afterwards the farmers found them –
the wasted young, turning up under their plough blades
as they tended the land back into itself.

Emotive word suggests they were not expecting them to be there.

Suggests that the poet considers the soldiers saintly for what they did.

5 A chit of bone, the china plate of a shoulder blade,
the relic of a finger, the blown
and broken bird's egg of a skull,

The metaphor makes it sound precious.

Fragile and delicate.

Links the past with the present where all that is left of them is their graves.

all mimicked now in flint, breaking blue in white
across this field where they were told to walk, not run,
towards the wood and its nesting machine guns.

Makes them sound natural which is juxtaposed with the danger they posed.

Suggests they were treated like children. The fact that they followed the order was what got them killed.

10 And even now the earth stands sentinel,
reaching back into itself for reminders of what happened
like a wound working a foreign body to the surface of the skin.

The only way these soldiers are remembered is by the actions of the land.

Present tense: the effects of conflict are still felt, and may reflect the idea that conflict is on-going in the world.

This morning, twenty men buried in one long grave,
a broken mosaic of bone linked arm in arm,
15 their skeletons paused mid dance-macabre

Shows the horror by the scale of the number of bodies in one grave. They were not given a proper burial.

The soldiers were comrades in life and joined in death.

Shocking imagery reminds the reader of the horrors that they witnessed.

in boots that outlasted them,
their socketed heads tilted back at an angle
and their jaws, those that have them, dropped open.

Contemplative tone as the poet considers the waste of life caused by conflict.

As if the notes they had sung
20 have only now, with this unearthing,
slipped from their absent tongues.

Key Features

| Metaphor | Simile | Personification | Emotive language |

About the Poem

- Written by **Owen Sheers** (1974–).

- The poem opens by describing how farmers 'found them' – the remains of soldiers who died during World War One.

- The poet writes about the waste of life through the imagery of the broken bones coming back to the surface many years later.

- The poem is based on a real incident. The battle was meant to last a few hours, but lasted for 5 days. Hundreds of soldiers died.

Ideas, Themes and Issues

- **Reality of conflict**: The poem uses shocking imagery to show the reality of war and the way in which the soldiers died.

- **Memory**: Not only is the poem about a specific memory, it is also a commemoration of the lives of the soldiers.

Form, Structure and Language

- The poem is set in a very **specific location** to emphasise that it really happened.

- The use of **metaphor** to describe the bones makes them seem precious and delicate. This emphasises that the soldiers' deaths were a waste.

- The **personification** of the earth is used in a range of ways: it suggests that it too was harmed by the war; that it was the only thing to memorialise the soldiers; as a sign of healing.

- The **shocking imagery** of the skeletons shows the horror of war.

- The use of the **simile** in line 12 has a **dual meaning**. It could be suggesting that the earth wants to be rid of the foreign bones, or reminding the living that the dead are there.

- The final **stanza** has a **contemplative** mood. The reference to 'absent tongues' suggests that they were ignored in life and that the soldiers' lives were wasted.

- The poem is **chronological**. This reminds us that even though this war was long ago, the repercussions are still felt today.

Quick Test

1. How does the poet show his feelings about conflict?

2. What evidence can you find that the soldiers were not adequately prepared for the battle?

3. What does the poet suggest about how people in the present view long-ago conflict?

Stanza • Contemplative • Chronological

The Yellow Palm

About the Poem

- Written by **Robert Minhinnick** (1952–).

- The poem was inspired by a visit to Iraq. It opens with the speaker describing what he sees as he walks through the streets of Baghdad.

- At first, the things that he notices seem calm and peaceful but he becomes aware of a more unpleasant and violent side to the city.

- At the end of the poem, the reader is left to decide whether they think there is a positive or a negative outcome.

- Although this is a poem about a specific conflict, it could be read as a comment on conflict in general.

Ideas, Themes and Issues

- **Reality of conflict**: The poem describes the impact that being involved in a conflict has on the place and the people involved. It shows that although not everything is violent, there is always the threat of violence to contend with.

- **Conflict affecting the individual**: With the exception of the blind beggars, the victims in this poem seem to be civilians. The poet is commenting on the idea that conflict has a profound effect on everyone, not just on soldiers.

The Yellow Palm

A symbol of love and mourning.

As I made my way down Palestine Street
I watched a funeral pass –
all the women waving lilac stems
around a coffin made of glass
5 and the face of the man who lay within
who had breathed a poison gas.

As I made my way down Palestine Street
I heard the call to prayer
and I stopped at the door of the golden mosque
10 to watch the faithful there
but there was blood on the walls and the muezzin's eye
were wild with his despair.

Juxtaposition of religious peace with violence and pain shows the horror of conflict.

As I made my way down Palestine Street
I met two blind beggars
15 And into their hands I pressed my hands
with a hundred black dinars;
and their salutes were those of the Imperial Guard
in the Mother of all Wars.

Key Features

| Shocking images | Religious imagery | Personification |

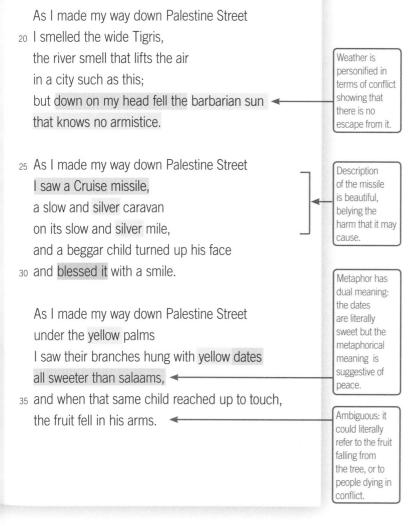

As I made my way down Palestine Street
20 I smelled the wide Tigris,
the river smell that lifts the air
in a city such as this;
but down on my head fell the barbarian sun
that knows no armistice.

> Weather is personified in terms of conflict showing that there is no escape from it.

25 As I made my way down Palestine Street
I saw a Cruise missile,
a slow and silver caravan
on its slow and silver mile,
and a beggar child turned up his face
30 and blessed it with a smile.

> Description of the missile is beautiful, belying the harm that it may cause.

As I made my way down Palestine Street
under the yellow palms
I saw their branches hung with yellow dates
all sweeter than salaams,
35 and when that same child reached up to touch,
the fruit fell in his arms.

> Metaphor has dual meaning: the dates are literally sweet but the metaphorical meaning is suggestive of peace.

> Ambiguous: it could literally refer to the fruit falling from the tree, or to people dying in conflict.

Colour   Metaphor

Form, Structure and Language

- The poem is written in the **first person**. It draws the reader into the action by describing the place vividly.

- Each **stanza** contains a **positive image** juxtaposed with a **shocking image** to emphasise that conflict has an impact far beyond the battlefield.

- The **personification** of the weather emphasises that conflict is **relentless**.

- The description of the missile is **contradictory**: something devastating is described in a positive way to reflect the confusion caused by the events that have taken place.

- **Religious imagery** reminds the reader that religious belief is important in the lives of the people, but that conflict is not respectful of that.

- References to **colour** help to create a sense that the place is bright and vibrant. At first glance, it doesn't seem like a place affected by conflict.

- The ending is **ambiguous**, leaving the reader to consider the likely outcome of this conflict.

Quick Test

1. What does the poet suggest about the daily lives of the people in Baghdad?

2. How does the poet show his feelings about conflict?

3. At the end of the poem, do you think the poet has hope for the future?

Personification • Imagery • Ambiguous

Key Words   11

The Right Word

About the Poem

- Written by **Imtiaz Dharker** (1954–).

- The poem opens with the poet wondering what terminology she should use to describe the person outside the door.

- She considers a variety of words before concluding that the person is just a child.

- The threat is diminished when she acknowledges that none of the words are 'the right word' and people realise that the person is just like them.

- The poem is a comment on the way people use language, and how this can exacerbate conflict. In the poem, people never seem to be able to find 'the right word'.

- The voice of the poet is clear in the poem. This is an issue that she feels strongly about.

Ideas, Themes and Issues

- **Reality of conflict**: Explores the idea that conflict is often caused or made worse by the language that people use to describe others.

- **Anti-war:** Suggests that if we all thought more about what we said, we might be able to avoid conflict.

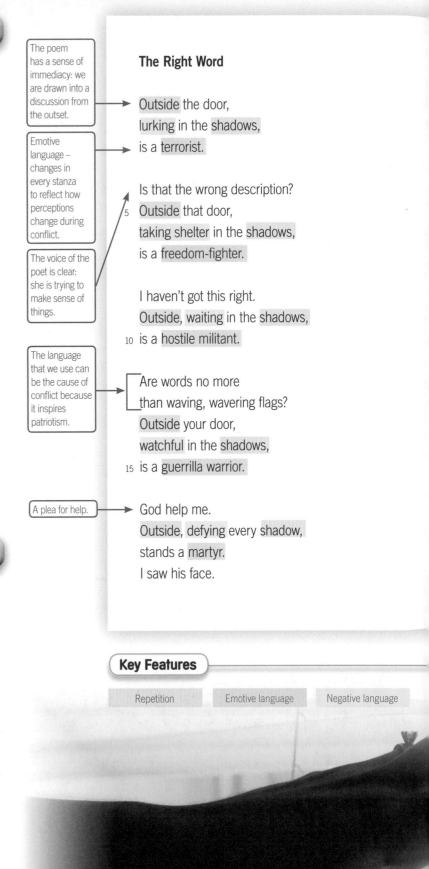

The poem has a sense of immediacy: we are drawn into a discussion from the outset.

Emotive language – changes in every stanza to reflect how perceptions change during conflict.

The voice of the poet is clear: she is trying to make sense of things.

The language that we use can be the cause of conflict because it inspires patriotism.

A plea for help.

The Right Word

Outside the door,
lurking in the shadows,
is a terrorist.

Is that the wrong description?
5   Outside that door,
taking shelter in the shadows,
is a freedom-fighter.

I haven't got this right.
Outside, waiting in the shadows,
10 is a hostile militant.

Are words no more
than waving, wavering flags?
Outside your door,
watchful in the shadows,
15 is a guerrilla warrior.

God help me.
Outside, defying every shadow,
stands a martyr.
I saw his face.

Key Features

| Repetition | Emotive language | Negative language |

Present tense • Pejorative language

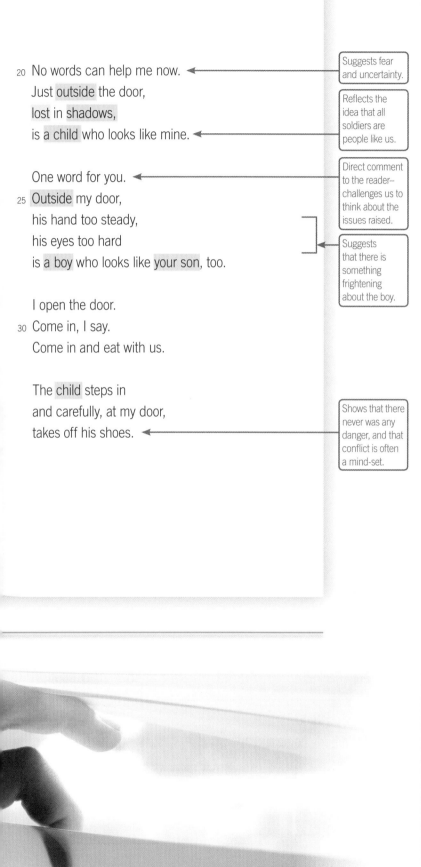

20 No words can help me now.
Just outside the door,
lost in shadows,
is a child who looks like mine.

One word for you.
25 Outside my door,
his hand too steady,
his eyes too hard
is a boy who looks like your son, too.

I open the door.
30 Come in, I say.
Come in and eat with us.

The child steps in
and carefully, at my door,
takes off his shoes.

Suggests fear and uncertainty.

Reflects the idea that all soldiers are people like us.

Direct comment to the reader— challenges us to think about the issues raised.

Suggests that there is something frightening about the boy.

Shows that there never was any danger, and that conflict is often a mind-set.

Form, Structure and Language

- The use of the **present tense** makes it clear that this is about conflict that is happening today, and is on-going.

- **Pejorative language** describes the person 'outside' suggesting that people are often quick to judge and their perceptions are negative.

- The language used is **emotive**, showing how language and conflict are emotive topics.

- The reference to flags, a **symbol of patriotism**, suggests that language is linked to identity which can lead to conflict.

- **Repetition** of the word 'shadows' suggests there are many things which are unclear to people, which can cause fear and conflict. The shadows are both literal and metaphorical.

- **Repetition** of 'outside' suggests that people don't always understand things that they haven't experienced first-hand.

- The use of the **pronoun** 'you' draws the reader into the poem, challenging us to rethink our ideas about language.

Quick Test

1. What does the poet consider to be a cause of conflict?

2. How does the poet use language to show her feelings about the cause of conflict?

3. Does the poet see any hope for the future?

At the Border, 1979

Sets it at a specific time and place.

At the Border, 1979

'It is your last check-in point in this country!'
We grabbed a drink –
soon everything would taste different.

This is what the children have been told.

Direct speech gives the poem a sense of immediacy. Appears to be the climax of their journey.

The land under our feet continued
5   divided by a thick iron chain.

Suggests that the border is physically very insignificant. It is manmade.

My sister put her leg across it.
'Look over here,' she said to us,
'my right leg is in this country
and my left leg in the other.'
10 The border guards told her off.

Suggests that they are the ones in control.

My mother informed me: *We are going home.*
She said that the roads are much cleaner
the landscape is more beautiful
and people are much kinder.

It is unclear until the fourth stanza that they are returning 'home'. 'Home' is an emotive word.

15 Dozens of families waited in the rain.
'I can inhale home,' somebody said.
Now our mothers were crying. I was five years old
standing by the check-in point
comparing both sides of the border.

Child's view of the border is very different from the adult's view.

20 The autumn soil continued on the other side
with the same colour, the same texture.
It rained on both sides of the chain.

We waited while our papers were checked,
our faces thoroughly inspected.
25 Then the chain was removed to let us through.
A man bent down and kissed his muddy homeland.
The same chain of mountains encompassed all of us.

They are at the mercy of the border guards.

Dual meaning: the mountains physically surround all of these people but also reflects idea that physical borders are meaningless.

Key Features

Difference   Similarity   Urgency   Emotive

About the Poem

- Written by **Choman Hardi** (1974–).

- The **first person** narrator recalls the time when she and her family crossed the border between Iran and Iraq at the age of 5.

- She describes the responses of various people at the border crossing, including herself and her sister, and the adults in the group.

- Although the event really happened, she deliberately doesn't specify a single event. This means that the poem is about borders and divides in a more general way.

Ideas, Themes and Issues

- **Patriotism**: The poem considers what 'home' is and what it means to different people. It also considers how people think about their home.

- **Symbols of conflict**: The poem considers the nature of borders and how they affect people. The border in the poem is physically insignificant, but has a great deal of meaning to people. The chain is something real and, at the same time, symbolic.

Form, Structure and Language

- The poem is written in the **first person** showing that this is a memory of a real event.

- **Direct speech** at the start of the poem gives a sense of **immediacy** which makes it seem as if we have joined the story part way through.

- There is a sense of **urgency** in the use of the verb 'grabbed'. It makes it sound as though they are eager to cross the border.

- **Emotive** language shows the reader that crossing a border is not a simple act, but an emotional one.

- **Hyperbole** is used to show the strength of feeling of the different people in the poem.

- The **semantic field** of **similarity** is **juxtaposed** with a semantic field of **difference**. In reality the land on both sides of the border is the same, but people's feelings about the land are very different. There is a clear **paradox** in lines 4 and 5 which emphasises this.

- The last line of the poem has a **dual meaning** showing that land and identity are clearly linked, and that borders are meaningless.

Quick Test

1. What is the difference between the way in which the adults see the border, and the way the children see it?

2. How does the poet use language to show this difference?

3. How do the ideas in this poem link with the theme of 'conflict'?

Belfast Confetti

A euphemism for a bomb.

The reader is placed at the centre of the action.

Some homemade bombs were filled with items like this.

Onomatopoeia reflects the sound of gunfire. Also linked to the persona's fear.

Accumulation of names and places from Colonial history is a reminder of past conflicts. The streets have been named after them.

Accumulation of jargon shows that these things are familiar to the persona. However, the language is unfamiliar and frightening to the reader.

Ironic. Confetti is normally used in celebration.

The use of enjambment foregrounds the words on this line.

Ellipsis suggests the sound of gunfire.

Accumulation of questions suggests confusion, but also relates to the idea that everyone in Belfast is under suspicion.

Belfast Confetti

Suddenly as the riot squad moved in it was raining exclamation
  marks,
Nuts, bolts, nails, car-keys. A fount of broken type. And
  the explosion
5 Itself – an asterisk on the map. This hyphenated line, a burst
  of rapid fire …
I was trying to complete a sentence in my head, but it kept
  stuttering,
All the alleyways and side streets blocked with stops and
10 colons.

I know this labyrinth so well – Balaklava, Raglan, Inkerman,
  Odessa Street –
Why can't I escape? Every move is punctuated. Crimea Street.
  Dead end again.
15 A Saracen, Kremlin-2 mesh. Makrolon face-shields. Walkie-
  talkies. What is
My name? Where am I coming from? Where am I going?
  A fusillade of question-marks.

Key Features

Accumulation   Reference to punctuation   Onomatopoeia

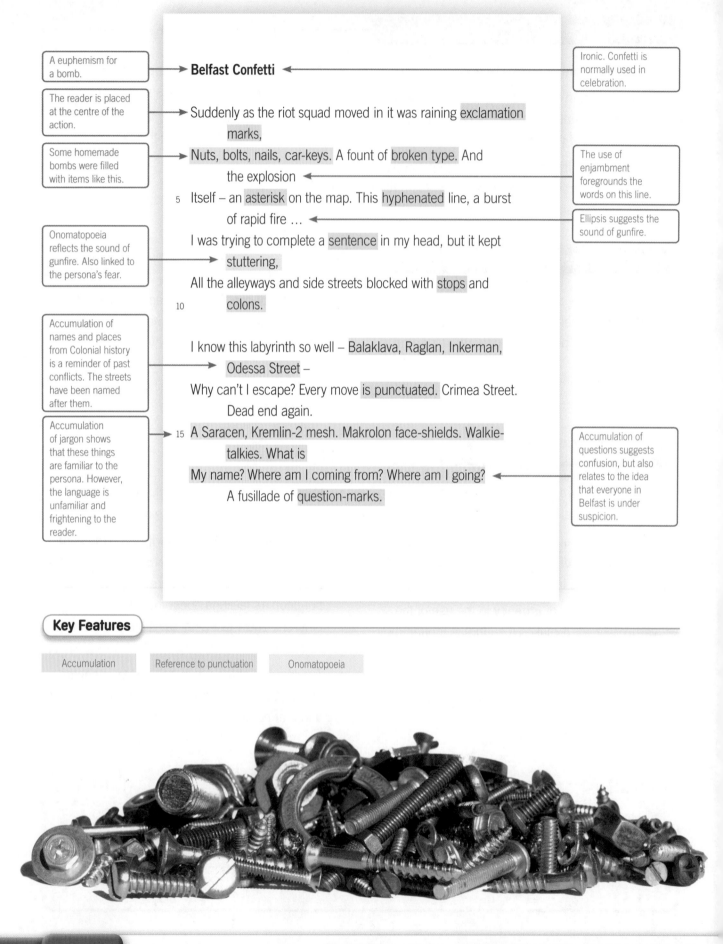

Euphemism • Irony • Accumulation • Ellipsis • Onomatopoeia

About the Poem

- Written by **Ciaran Carson** (1948–).

- The poem opens as a bomb goes off in the city. The persona is caught up in it and tries to get away.

- As he tries to escape, all of his routes are blocked and he is thrown into a sense of confusion and panic.

- He is stopped and questioned by the security forces.

- As well as being about a particular incident, this poem could also be about the Troubles in Northern Ireland in general, and how it felt to be caught up in them.

Ideas, Themes and Issues

- **Reality of war**: The vivid description of the bomb going off as well as the effects of that shows the reality of life during the Troubles.

- **Conflict affecting the individual**: Shows how conflict affects the ordinary people who are involved, rather than the soldiers.

Form, Structure and Language

- There is a sense of **immediacy** as the poem opens just as a bomb explodes.

- The title of the poem is a **euphemistic** term for a bomb. It is **ironic** that something normally linked with ideas of celebration is linked to a bomb.

- The **accumulation** of items inside the bomb suggests how ferocious it was. This technique is used throughout the poem to emphasise the confusion caused by the bomb.

- **Reference to punctuation** shows the content of the bomb, and that everyday life is punctuated by events such as these. It also suggests that language is a cause of conflict, and a possible solution to it.

- The **ellipsis** in line 6 and **onomatopoeia** in line 8 reflect the sounds of gunfire.

- **Enjambment** throughout the poem shows how quickly things happened. It **foregrounds** words like 'explosion' by putting them on new lines.

- Military **jargon** in the second **stanza** emphasises how frightening and unfamiliar life is when conflict is taking place. The **questions** at the end of the poem support this idea.

- The **shape** of the poem is unusual. The different line lengths suggest that the poet is finding it hard to think with all the chaos around him.

Quick Test

1. How does the writer feel about being caught up in conflict?

2. How does the writer show these feelings in the poem?

3. Do you think this poem is simply about the Troubles?

Poppies

About the Poem

- Written by **Jane Weir** (1963–).

- The poem opens with a mother describing the day her son leaves home to join the army.

- It is just before Armistice Sunday, and there are already poppies on graves in the local cemetery.

- She pins one to her son's uniform and then helps him to get ready to leave, controlling her emotions as she tidies his uniform for him.

- After he has gone, she is able to release her emotions by going to places that remind her of him.

Ideas, Themes and Issues

- **Women and conflict**: Explores the feelings of a woman left behind, and reminds the reader that this was a reality for many women in past wars.

- **Symbols of conflict**: There are references throughout the poem to symbols of conflict, such as the poppy and the dove.

Opens with an ominous reminder of the effects of conflict since poppies are symbolic of those who have died at war.

Dual meaning: the petals are literally 'crimped' i.e. bent, but it also means to recruit someone into the army under false pretences.

Alliteration emphasises her attempt to control her emotions.

Metaphor suggests that he is too grown up to want signs of affection from his mother.

Poppies

Three days before Armistice Sunday
and poppies had already been placed
on individual war graves. Before you left,
I pinned one onto your lapel, crimped petals,
5 spasms of paper red, disrupting a blockade
of yellow bias binding around your blazer.

Sellotape bandaged around my hand,
I rounded up as many white cat hairs
as I could, smoothed down your shirt's
10 upturned collar, steeled the softening
of my face. I wanted to graze my nose
across the tip of your nose, play at
being Eskimos like we did when
you were little. I resisted the impulse
15 to run my fingers through the gelled
blackthorns of your hair. All my words
flattened, rolled, turned into felt,

Key Features

Metaphor   Simile   Maternal love

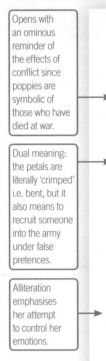

     Dramatic monologue • First person • Lament • Juxtaposition

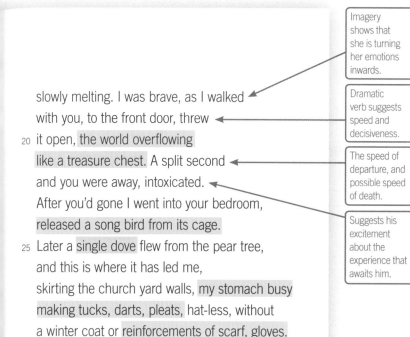

Imagery shows that she is turning her emotions inwards.

Dramatic verb suggests speed and decisiveness.

The speed of departure, and possible speed of death.

Suggests his excitement about the experience that awaits him.

slowly melting. I was brave, as I walked
with you, to the front door, threw
20 it open, the world overflowing
like a treasure chest. A split second
and you were away, intoxicated.
After you'd gone I went into your bedroom,
released a song bird from its cage.

25 Later a single dove flew from the pear tree,
and this is where it has led me,
skirting the church yard walls, my stomach busy
making tucks, darts, pleats, hat-less, without
a winter coat or reinforcements of scarf, gloves.

30 On reaching the top of the hill I traced
the inscriptions on the war memorial,
leaned against it like a wishbone.
The dove pulled freely against the sky,
an ornamental stitch. I listened, hoping to hear
35 your playground voice catching on the wind.

Suggests that this is a way of wishing her son safely home.

Reference to his childhood. This also links to the ideas in lines 11–14.

Pain and danger   War and peace

Form, Structure and Language

- The poem is a **dramatic monologue** written in the **first person**. This shows the emotions of the persona. It is a **lament** for the loss of her son.

- The **juxtaposition** of the victims in the war graves and the persona's son in lines 3 and 4 evokes an emotional response from the reader. Use of **simile** and **metaphor** also help to develop this.

- **Everyday** imagery at the beginning of the second stanza emphasises that soldiers are normal people. This contrasts with **imagery of war**.

- The paradox in lines 20 and 21 suggests hope and promise but this is not the feeling the mother has.

- There is a **semantic field of maternal love** to show how difficult it must be to let a child go to war. This contrasts with **imagery of physical pain and danger**.

- **References to childhood,** as in lines 34 and 35, are a reminder that every soldier is someone's son.

- The poem is **ambiguous**: it is not clear whether her son is one of the dead in the 'war graves'.

Quick Test

1. How does the poet show feelings about conflict in the poem?
2. What does the poet suggest conflict is like for those left behind?
3. What do the songbird and the dove represent?

Simile • Metaphor • Imagery • Semantic field • Ambiguous

Futility

Title sets the negative mood from the start.

Futility

Move him into the sun –
Gently its touch awoke him once,
At home, whispering of fields half-sown.
Always it woke him, even in France,
5 Until this morning and this snow.
If anything might rouse him now
The kind old sun will know.

Think how it wakes the seeds –
Woke once the clays of a cold star.
10 Are limbs, so dear achieved, are sides
Full-nerved, still warm, too hard to stir?
Was it for this the clay grew tall?
– O what made fatuous sunbeams toil
To break earth's sleep at all?

Imperative suggests that he can't move himself.

Personification of the sun suggests that nature is powerful.

Ironic that the sun is personified in this way, since even it can't help him now.

This interjection sounds like a cry of pain.

Dual meaning: refers to literal fields that he may have been responsible for, but also to the youth of the soldiers.

Imagery of cold is juxtaposed with the imagery of the sun to show the contrast between life and death.

Suggests that trying to wake him is futile, and links to the title.

Emotive language reminds us that he has only just died.

Shows his anger at the waste of life.

Key Features

| Warm images | Cold images | Time | Questions | Imperative |

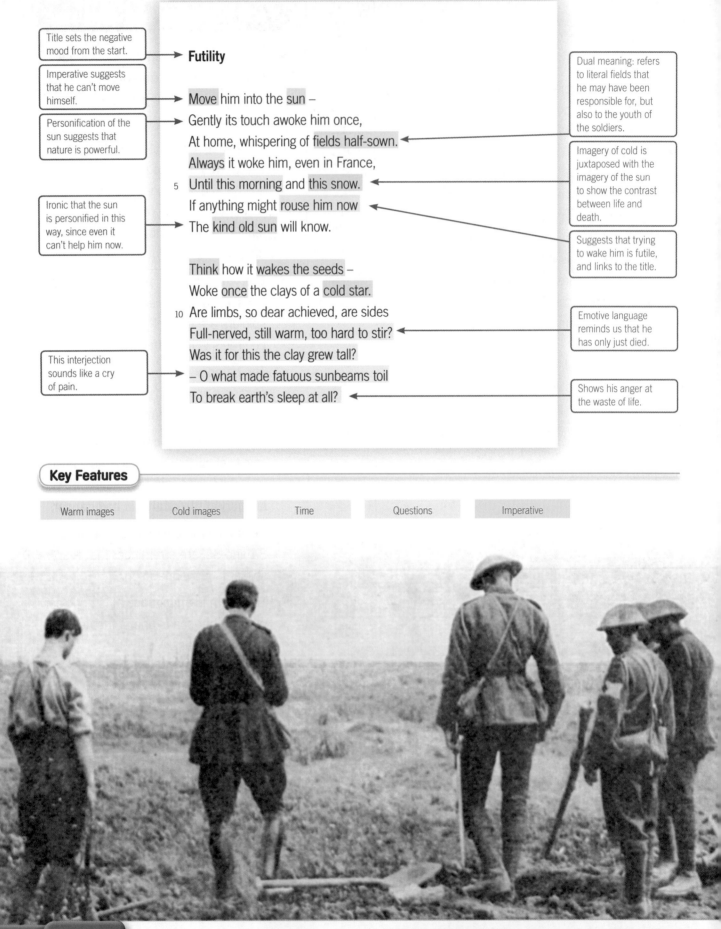

Sonnet • First person • Imperative • Personification

About the Poem

- Written by **Wilfred Owen** (1893–1918).
- Owen served in World War One and died just a week before the end of the war. His poems are written from personal experience.

- It opens with the persona telling other soldiers to move a dead comrade into the sun in the vain hope that it will wake him.
- The poem describes the pointlessness of war.

Ideas, Themes and Issues

- **Grief**: The poet expresses his feeling of loss at the death of a comrade.
- **Anti-war message**: Considers the pointlessness of life if conflict results in loss of life.

- **Effect on the individual**: Although the poem seems to focus on the death of one solider, its wider message is about the death of humanity.

Form, Structure and Language

- The poem is a **sonnet**. It is a love poem for those who have died in conflict.
- The poem is written in the **first person**. We're not told who 'him' is, so it could be about a personal experience or conflict in general.
- The **imperative** in the first line is a command, yet the **tone is gentle** and caring, which seems at odds with conflict. Another imperative is used in line 8, which forces the reader to **think** about the message of the poem.
- **Personification** is used to show the **power of nature** but the poet shows that even nature is no match for military conflict.
- The **warm images** of the sun are **juxtaposed** with **images of cold**. This suggests the contrast between life and death.

- **References to time** suggest that time has run out for the soldier.
- **Emotive language** shows the poet's feelings about war, and evokes an emotional response from the reader.
- The **interjection** in line 13 sounds like a cry of pain or sorrow, and emphasises the **tragedy** of war. This could also reflect the fact that the poet's experiences in war made him question his **religion**.
- The **questions** in the second **stanza** suggest that the persona is questioning the point of conflict, and also encourage the reader to do so.

Quick Test

1. What does the poet consider to be futile?
2. How does the poet use language to show 'Futility'?
3. The poet doesn't describe a battle in the poem. Do you think this makes it more or less effective at portraying war?

The Charge of the Light Brigade

About the Poem

- Written by **Alfred, Lord Tennyson** (1809–1892).

- Based on a real event in the Crimean War, the poem was inspired by an account of the battle that Tennyson read.

- The poem opens at the start of the charge, and describes how the cavalry fearlessly ride into battle.

- There has been a mistake with the order, but despite the fact that they have fewer men and poorer weapons than the enemy, the patriotic cavalry ride on regardless.

- Tennyson vividly describes how bravely they fought, and the losses they sustained.

- At the end of the poem, he calls for them to be remembered for their bravery.

Ideas, Themes and Issues

- **Patriotism**: The cavalry soldiers are undoubtedly patriotic and Tennyson celebrates their bravery in the face of immense danger throughout the poem.

- **Memory**: The poem is a vivid evocation of a past battle and reminds the reader of the reality of past conflicts. It remembers and celebrates the brave actions of those who have died in conflict.

The Charge of the Light Brigade

Reference to the Bible as well as personification of the place, which makes it seem more threatening.

Rhyme scheme varies throughout the poem.

Repetition emphasises that the patriotic soldiers didn't challenge the order.

Repetition shows that the soldiers kept going in the face of all danger.

Accumulation emphasises that they were outnumbered.

Onomatopoeia evokes the sound of the battle.

1.
Half a league, half a league,
Half a league onward,
All in the valley of Death
    Rode the six hundred.
5 'Forward, the Light Brigade!
Charge for the guns!' he said:
Into the valley of Death
    Rode the six hundred.

2.
'Forward, the Light Brigade!'
10 Was there a man dismay'd?
Not tho' the soldier knew
    Some one had blunder'd:
Theirs not to make reply,
Theirs not to reason why,
15 Theirs but to do and die:
Into the valley of Death
    Rode the six hundred.

3.
Cannon to right of them,
Cannon to left of them,
20 Cannon in front of them
    Volley'd and thunder'd;
Storm'd at with shot and shell,
Boldly they rode and well,
Into the jaws of Death,
25 Into the mouth of Hell
    Rode the six hundred.

Key Features

| Repetition | Negative language | Pride |

Third person • Rhythm • Stanza • Rhyme • Foreground

4.

Flash'd all their sabres bare,
Flash'd as they turn'd in air
Sabring the gunners there,
30 Charging an army, while
   All the world wonder'd:
Plunged in the battery-smoke
Right thro' the line they broke;
Cossack and Russian
35 Reel'd from the sabre-stroke
   Shatter'd and sunder'd.
Then they rode back, but not
   Not the six hundred.

5.

Cannon to right of them,
40 Cannon to left of them,
Cannon behind them
   Volley'd and thunder'd;
Storm'd at with shot and shell,
While horse and hero fell,
45 They that had fought so well
Came thro' the jaws of Death
Back from the mouth of Hell,
All that was left of them
   Left of six hundred.

6.

50 When can their glory fade?
   O the wild charge they made!
   All the world wonder'd.
Honour the charge they made!
Honour the Light Brigade,
55   Noble six hundred!

The pride here comes from their refusal to be beaten, shown by the repetition. They are outclassed and outnumbered but they still go on.

Shows patriotic pride in their actions against the enemy.

Repetition emphasises that they didn't all return. There is a sense of sadness. This is the turning point in the poem.

Rhetorical question forces the reader to consider the bravery of their actions.

Hyperbolic statement.

Final line sums up Tennyson's view of the soldiers.

Rhyme

Form, Structure and Language

- The poem is written in the **third person** – the voice seems to be that of Tennyson writing about the event that he has read about.
- The poem is very **rhythmic** and as you read it aloud it is evocative of the **sound of the hoof beats**. The rhythm changes in **stanza** 2, and disappears altogether in stanza 6.
- **Rhyme** is used to help to **foreground** some of the key ideas in the poem.
- **References to the Bible** and **personification** emphasise the danger that the cavalry face.
- The use of **direct speech** in line 6 reminds us that these were real soldiers in a real battle. This helps to evoke a strong emotional response in the reader.
- The **accumulation** of images of cannon reflects that the soldiers were outnumbered.
- There is a **semantic field of pride** to show Tennyson's feelings about the actions of the soldiers.
- **The final stanza is the shortest**, which may reflect that the soldiers' lives were cut tragically short.

Quick Test

1 How does the poet suggest his admiration for the soldiers?
2 How does the poet suggest the reality of battle?
3 What is the effect of the short final stanza?

Personification • Direct speech • Accumulation • Semantic field   **Key Words** 23

Bayonet Charge

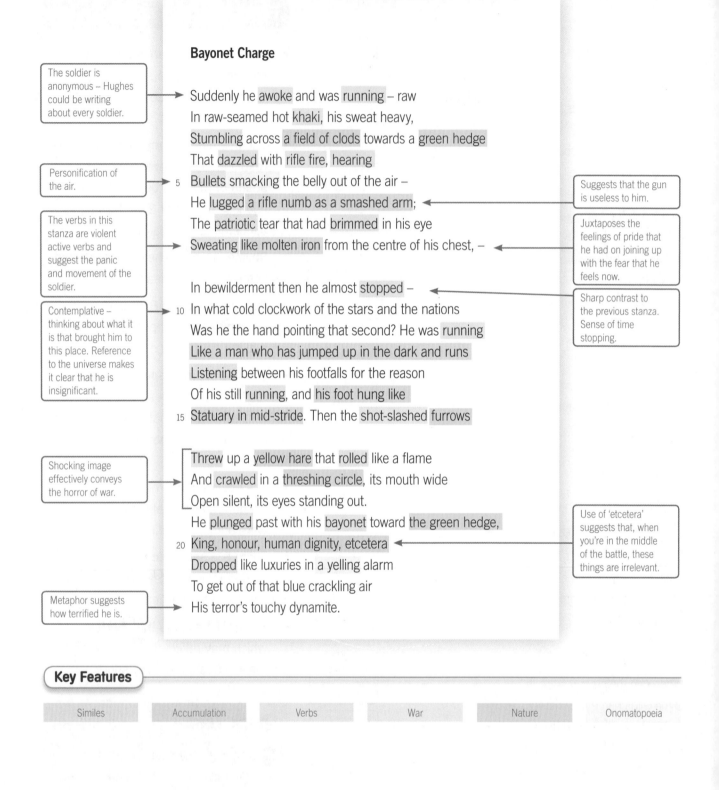

Bayonet Charge

The soldier is anonymous – Hughes could be writing about every soldier.

Personification of the air.

The verbs in this stanza are violent active verbs and suggest the panic and movement of the soldier.

Contemplative – thinking about what it is that brought him to this place. Reference to the universe makes it clear that he is insignificant.

Shocking image effectively conveys the horror of war.

Metaphor suggests how terrified he is.

Suggests that the gun is useless to him.

Juxtaposes the feelings of pride that he had on joining up with the fear that he feels now.

Sharp contrast to the previous stanza. Sense of time stopping.

Use of 'etcetera' suggests that, when you're in the middle of the battle, these things are irrelevant.

Suddenly he awoke and was running – raw
In raw-seamed hot khaki, his sweat heavy,
Stumbling across a field of clods towards a green hedge
That dazzled with rifle fire, hearing
5 Bullets smacking the belly out of the air –
He lugged a rifle numb as a smashed arm;
The patriotic tear that had brimmed in his eye
Sweating like molten iron from the centre of his chest, –

In bewilderment then he almost stopped –
10 In what cold clockwork of the stars and the nations
Was he the hand pointing that second? He was running
Like a man who has jumped up in the dark and runs
Listening between his footfalls for the reason
Of his still running, and his foot hung like
15 Statuary in mid-stride. Then the shot-slashed furrows

Threw up a yellow hare that rolled like a flame
And crawled in a threshing circle, its mouth wide
Open silent, its eyes standing out.
He plunged past with his bayonet toward the green hedge,
20 King, honour, human dignity, etcetera
Dropped like luxuries in a yelling alarm
To get out of that blue crackling air
His terror's touchy dynamite.

Key Features

Similes   Accumulation   Verbs   War   Nature   Onomatopoeia

About the Poem

- Written by **Ted Hughes** (1930–1998).

- The poem opens with the narrator describing the terrified actions of the soldier as he runs across the battlefield making the bayonet charge.

- For a moment, he thinks about what it is that has brought him to this time and place, before a horrifying image of death brings him back to reality.

- The soldier is not named: the poet's choice to make him anonymous makes him represent all soldiers.

Ideas, Themes and Issues

- **Reality of war**: Vividly describes the events of the battle, showing their wider impact.

- **Patriotism**: In line 20, the poet suggests that the motives that people claim for going to war are luxuries which have no place in the reality of war.

Form, Structure and Language

- **Verbs** give a clear sense of the **movement** in the poem. It feels frantic as the soldier makes his charge. Many of the verbs suggest that he isn't in control of the situation.

- There are only four sentences in the whole poem, which use **enjambment** to add to the sense of movement and further reflect his lack of control.

- The **personification** of the air in line 5 shows the violence of the bullets, and suggests that they are everywhere.

- **Onomatopoeia** is used to convey the sounds of the battlefield.

- The second **stanza** opens in a more **contemplative** way. The phrase 'almost stopped' has a **dual meaning**: it could refer to his physically stopping, or to his mentally stopping to think about war.

- The use of **accumulation** in line 20 shows that there are many reasons for going to war, but all of them seem irrelevant when a person is in the middle of it.

- **Semantic fields** of **war and nature** are **juxtaposed** showing the impact of war on land.

- The poem is a snapshot of a single moment on the battlefield. This suggests that the events are so powerful that they will never leave the soldier.

Quick Test

1. How does the poet show that the battle is raging around the soldier?

2. What does the poet think about war?

3. How does the poet show his feelings about war?

Contemplative • Accumulation • Semantic field • Juxtaposition

The Falling Leaves

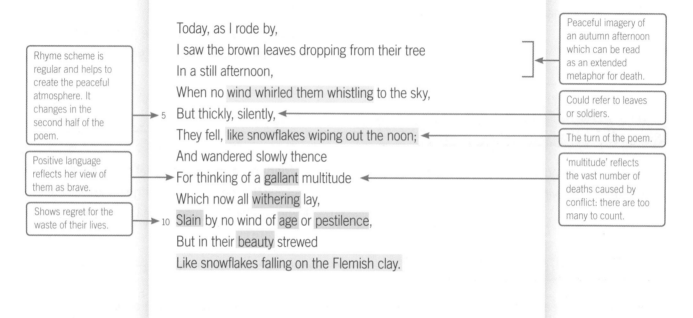

The Falling Leaves

November 1915

Today, as I rode by,
I saw the brown leaves dropping from their tree
In a still afternoon,
When no wind whirled them whistling to the sky,
5 But thickly, silently,
They fell, like snowflakes wiping out the noon;
And wandered slowly thence
For thinking of a gallant multitude
Which now all withering lay,
10 Slain by no wind of age or pestilence,
But in their beauty strewed
Like snowflakes falling on the Flemish clay.

Annotations:

Rhyme scheme is regular and helps to create the peaceful atmosphere. It changes in the second half of the poem.

Positive language reflects her view of them as brave.

Shows regret for the waste of their lives.

Peaceful imagery of an autumn afternoon which can be read as an extended metaphor for death.

Could refer to leaves or soldiers.

The turn of the poem.

'multitude' reflects the vast number of deaths caused by conflict: there are too many to count.

Key Features

Positive language Negative language Simile Onomatopoeia/Alliteration

First person • Elegy • Rhyme • Half-rhyme • Imagery • Contemplative

About the Poem

- Written by **Margaret Postgate Cole** (1893–1980).

- The poem opens with the poet seeing leaves falling from a tree on a still Autumn day.

- This reminds her of the soldiers who died in the First World War.

Ideas, Themes and Issues

- **Grief**: The poet feels a sense of loss and waste at the deaths of young men in conflict. She feels that they have died before their time.

- **Respect**: There is a clear sense that the poet respects those who have died, although she doesn't celebrate their actions.

Form, Structure and Language

- The poem is in the **first person** which makes the reader feel that this is the poet's own response to conflict.

- The poem is an **elegy** for the dead. The poet's use of **rhyme** and **half-rhyme** helps to create this effect.

- The **peaceful imagery** of the opening sets the **contemplative** tone for a poem.

- The leaves are an **extended metaphor** for the soldiers; they remind the reader of the number of people who have died in conflict.

- **Onomatopoeia** and **alliteration** in line 4 help to evoke the stillness and calmness of the setting.

- The **consonance** of the **'w' sound** throughout the poem helps to develop the idea that the soldiers die unobtrusively.

- The **turn of the poem** in line 6 marks the point where the poet begins to see the leaves as a metaphor for the soldiers.

- The use of **similes** in lines 6 and 12 reflects the poet's train of thought as she looks at the leaves and thinks of the soldiers.

- **Negative language** is used to highlight the danger of conflict, whilst **positive language** is used to emphasise the poet's view of the bravery of the soldiers.

- There is a clear sense of **regret** as the poet contemplates the waste of life.

Quick Test

1. What does the poet feel about conflict?
2. How does the poet show these feelings?
3. Why do you think that the poet chose the metaphor of the falling leaves to reflect the soldiers?
4. What do you think is the significance of the snowflakes in the poem?

Extended metaphor • Onomatopoeia • Alliteration • Consonance • Simile

Key Words

'Come On, Come Back'

About the Poem

- Written by **Stevie Smith** (1902–1971).

- The poem is about a war in the future but contains references to a past war. A girl soldier called Vaudevue has been tortured and is sitting alone on the battlefield.

- She is so damaged by her experiences that she strips her uniform off and dives into an icy lake where she drowns.

- A passing soldier, in the enemy army, sees her clothes and waits for her. He plays a tune for her, not realising that she is already dead.

- The poem is **chronological**, starting with Vaudevue on the battlefield and ending with her death.

Ideas, Themes and Issues

- **Reality of conflict**: Considers the devastating impact that war can have on people.

- **Anti-war message**: At the end of the poem, it is her enemy who marks her death. This shows that war is essentially pointless since people are all the same.

- **Conflict affecting the individual**: Focuses on the effect of war on one person, but the poem also reflects ideas about all wars.

Metaphor refers to the battle going away. Tides also flow, which suggests that this is not a permanent situation.

The image of the 'girl soldier' is unexpected and shocking.

The contrast between her life and the death of her memory shows the shocking effect of conflict.

Dual meaning: relates to memory loss, but also a philosophical question to do with conflict and her role in it.

Shows that war can reduce grown men and women to a childlike state.

'Adorable' is a strange choice of word. Does this reflect the damage to her mind, or that this is her only relief from what has happened to her?

'Come On, Come Back'

Incident in a future war

Left by the ebbing tide of battle
On the field of Austerlitz
The girl soldier Vaudevue sits
Her fingers tap the ground, she is alone
5 At midnight in the moonlight she is sitting alone on a round flat stone.

Graded by the Memel Conference first
Of all human exterminators
M.L.5.
Has left her just alive
10 Only her memory is dead for evermore.
She fears and cries, Ah me why am I here?
Sitting alone on a round flat stone on a hummock there

Rising, staggering, over the ground she goes
Over the seeming miles of rutted meadow
15 To the margin of a lake
The sand beneath her feet
Is cold and damp and firm to the waves' beat.

Quickly – as a child, an idiot, as one without memory –
She strips her uniform off, strips, stands and plunges
20 Into the icy waters of the adorable lake.
On the surface of the water lies
A ribbon of white moonlight
The waters on either side of the moony track
Are black as her mind,
25 Her mind is as secret from her
As the water on which she swims,
As secret as profound as ominous.

Key Features

| Metaphor | Negative language | Positive language |

Chronological • Enjambment • Juxtaposition • Oxymoron • Alliteration

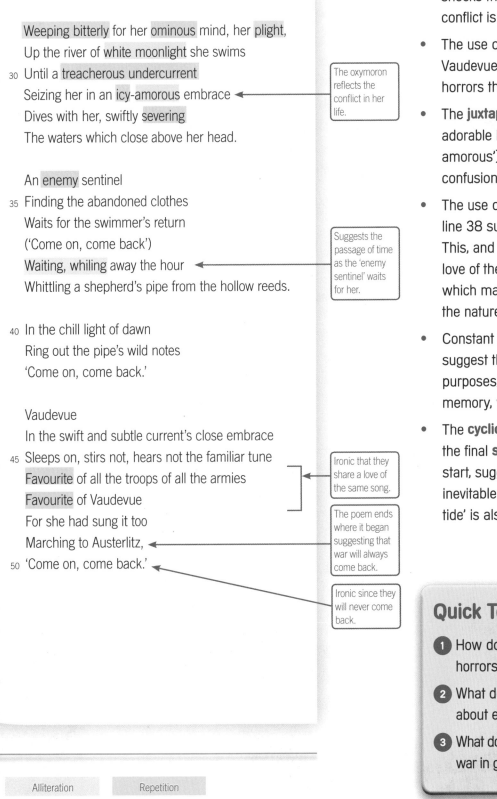

Weeping bitterly for her ominous mind, her plight,
Up the river of white moonlight she swims
30 Until a treacherous undercurrent
Seizing her in an icy-amorous embrace
Dives with her, swiftly severing
The waters which close above her head.

An enemy sentinel
35 Finding the abandoned clothes
Waits for the swimmer's return
('Come on, come back')
Waiting, whiling away the hour
Whittling a shepherd's pipe from the hollow reeds.

40 In the chill light of dawn
Ring out the pipe's wild notes
'Come on, come back.'

Vaudevue
In the swift and subtle current's close embrace
45 Sleeps on, stirs not, hears not the familiar tune
Favourite of all the troops of all the armies
Favourite of Vaudevue
For she had sung it too
Marching to Austerlitz,
50 'Come on, come back.'

The oxymoron reflects the conflict in her life.

Suggests the passage of time as the 'enemy sentinel' waits for her.

Ironic that they share a love of the same song.

The poem ends where it began suggesting that war will always come back.

Ironic since they will never come back.

Alliteration   Repetition

Form, Structure and Language

- The **unemotional language** used to describe 'human exterminators' shocks the reader and reminds us that conflict is brutal.

- The use of **enjambment** suggests Vaudevue's hurry to escape from the horrors that she has experienced.

- The **juxtaposition** ('icy waters of the adorable lake') and **oxymoron** ('icy-amorous') reflect the conflict and confusion in her life.

- The use of **alliteration** and **caesura** in line 38 suggests the passage of time. This, and the fact that they share a love of the same song, are **ironic**, which may reflect the poet's view of the nature of conflict.

- Constant **references to memory** suggest that she has, to all intents and purposes, already died. Without memory, we are without identity.

- The **cyclical** reference to **Austerlitz** in the final **stanza** takes us back to the start, suggesting that conflict is inevitable. The **metaphor** of the 'ebbing tide' is also a reminder of this.

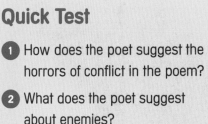

Quick Test

1 How does the poet suggest the horrors of conflict in the poem?

2 What does the poet suggest about enemies?

3 What does the poet suggest about war in general?

next to of course god america i

next to of course god america i

Speech marks suggest this is an account of a speech being retold.

"next to of course god america i
love you land of the pilgrims' and so forth oh
say can you see by the dawn's early my
country 'tis of centuries come and go

5 and are no more what of it we should worry
in every language even deafanddumb
thy sons acclaim your glorious name by gorry
by jingo by gee by gosh by gum
why talk of beauty what could be more beaut-

10 iful than these heroic happy dead
who rushed like lions to the roaring slaughter
they did not stop to think they died instead
then shall the voice of liberty be mute?"

He spoke. And drank rapidly a glass of water

Intertextual reference suggests respect and admiration for his country.

Mocking tone, as if the speaker is mocking the idea of patriotism.

The normal expression is 'like lambs to the slaughter' which means they are innocent. 'Lions' suggests they are complicit in conflict.

Ambiguous: could be suggesting that when the soldiers died, the voice of liberty died, or a call to arms.

American slang marks the turn in the poem: from here, the language becomes more cynical.

Break in 'beautiful' sounds as if he couldn't bring himself to say it, so challenges what he is saying. Also suggests that conflict destroys beauty.

The persona seems to be mocking the original speaker. The first capital letter in the poem. It might refer to someone the speaker considers to be a higher power; perhaps God or a leader.

Key Features

Intertextual reference	Dismissive language	Cliché	Emotive language	Personification	Simile

Dramatic monologue • First person • Intertextual reference • Parody

About the Poem

- Written by **e. e. cummings** (1894–1962).

- The poem opens in the form of a speech being given about America.

- To begin with, it seems patriotic but it soon becomes clear that it isn't.

- By the end of the poem, the tone has changed and the speaker's views are more cynical.

- In the last line, a second speaker describes the first speaker's final actions.

Ideas, Themes and Issues

- **Patriotism**: The poem is questioning unthinking patriotism and the effects that it can have.

- **Anti-war**: It clearly expresses an anti-war message by exploring the idea that war is not heroic.

Form, Structure and Language

- The poem is a **dramatic monologue** in the **first person** which makes it feel as though the reader is hearing the speech in real life.

- The opening has a sense of **immediacy,** as if we are joining a conversation midway through.

- The **intertextual references** to famous American songs, The Star Spangled Banner and America, suggest that the speaker is deeply patriotic.

- The use of **dismissive language** suggests he doesn't really respect it and shows that the poem is actually a **parody** of a patriotic speech.

- America is **personified** in the poem. This emphasises that it is a deeply patriotic nation.

- **Clichés** are used to suggest that the accepted view of patriotism is overused.

- The use of **oxymoron** in line 10 shows the persona's **cynicism** about a nation which makes blindly patriotic statements about the 'heroic happy dead'.

- The **simile** in line 11 is used to suggest courage but also inevitability. It shows how the speaker feels about such actions. **Emotive** language also emphasises the speaker's feelings.

- The **question mark** in line 13 is the first piece of punctuation. The speaker expects the reader to engage with the question.

- The **isolation** of the final line and the **change in speaker** forces the reader to question the state of mind of the speaker, and the possible repercussions of his actions.

Quick Test

1. How does the poet suggest that America is a patriotic place?

2. How does the poet use language to suggest that he thinks that patriotism is not a good thing?

3. The poem is a sonnet. Do you think it is a love poem for America or something else?

Personification • Cliché • Oxymoron • Simile • Emotive

Key Words

Hawk Roosting

Hawk Roosting

First and last lines are both monosyllabic making them assertive.

Suggests that the hawk considers itself superior because it is realistic even in its dreams.

Repetition shows the power of the bird with its natural weaponry.

I sit in the top of the wood, my eyes closed.
Inaction, no falsifying dream
Between my hooked head and hooked feet:
Or in sleep rehearse perfect kills and eat.

5   The convenience of the high trees!
The air's buoyancy and the sun's ray
Are of advantage to me;
And the earth's face upward for my inspection.

Foregrounds the idea that the hawk is the centre of everything.

Personification of the earth stresses the hawk's perceived power.

My feet are locked upon the rough bark.
10   It took the whole of Creation
To produce my foot, my each feather:
Now I hold Creation in my foot

Reference to God shows the arrogance of the hawk: it thinks it is better than God.

Or fly up, and revolve it all slowly –
I kill where I please because it is all mine.
15   There is no sophistry in my body:
My manners are tearing off heads –

Arrogant to think that it has ultimate power.

Suggests that the hawk is proud of his actions.

The allotment of death.
For the one path of my flight is direct
Through the bones of the living.
20   No arguments assert my right:

Suggests that the idea is simple. It doesn't need to justify its actions.

Dual meaning: that the sun is literally behind the hawk, or that the hawk considers itself more important than the sun.

The sun is behind me.
Nothing has changed since I began.
My eye has permitted no change.
I am going to keep things like this.

Key Features

The hawk's power   Personal pronouns   Violent imagery

Extended metaphor • Dramatic monologue • Personal pronoun

About the Poem

- Written by **Ted Hughes** (1930–1998).
- The poem is written in the voice, and from the viewpoint of, the hawk. It describes its vision of the world, in which the hawk is the centre.
- The poem describes the actions of the hawk in a cold and chilling way.
- The poem can be read as an **extended metaphor** for those who take their countries to war.

Ideas, Themes and Issues

- **Power**: The hawk is powerful and violent. The actions in the poem are brutal and chilling and suggest the consequences of power being used wrongly.
- **Arrogance**: The hawk believes that it has ultimate power and that having power is the only justification needed to use it. It could be seen to represent people who act as though they have ultimate power. Hughes himself felt that this poem gave nature a voice.

Form, Structure and Language

- The poem is a **dramatic monologue** which shows the reader the hawk's point of view.
- **Personal pronouns** are used throughout the poem to show the bird's view of his position in the world.
- **Enjambment** is used to suggest the movement and power of the hawk.
- In the second **stanza**, the fact that the short line ends with 'me' **foregrounds** the word to emphasise the idea that the hawk considers itself the centre of the universe.
- The earth is **personified** to show the power of the hawk over the earth.
- The poet makes **references to God** which help to show the hawk's arrogance.
- There is a mixture of **formal** and **brutal** language in the poem. These are **juxtaposed** to show the hawk's pride in his actions.
- **Simple statements** such as line 17 reflect the idea that the hawk is arrogant about the importance of its actions.

Quick Test

1. How does the poet show the hawk's arrogance?
2. What evidence is there that this poem might be about human leaders taking their countries to war?
3. Look closely at the last stanza. How does the poet suggest that the hawk might not be as powerful as it thinks?

Enjambment • Stanza • Foreground • Personification • Juxtaposition

About the Exam

What to Expect

The exam is divided into two sections, Section A and Section B. **Section A focuses on the poetry from the *Moon on the Tides* anthology** and Section B focuses on unseen poetry.

The poems in the *Moon on the Tides* anthology are divided into four clusters:
- **Character and voice**
- **Place**
- **Conflict**
- **Relationships**

Each cluster contains 15 poems. Some of these poems are from the **Literary Heritage** and some are **contemporary**, including poems from **different cultures**.

There will be a **choice of two questions** for each cluster. You must choose **one** of the questions to answer. The question will **name one poem** and ask you to **compare** it to a poem of your choice. The poem you choose must be from the **same cluster**.

Some poems will only be named on one tier:
- *Belfast Confetti, The Yellow Palm*, and *next to of course god america i* will only be named on the higher tier paper.
- *Flag, The Right Word* and *The Falling Leaves* will only be named on the foundation tier paper.

You will be given a copy of the anthology in the exam, but **it will not have any notes or annotations** on it.

What You Will Be Assessed On

In Section A you'll be assessed on how well you do the following:

AO1	**Respond to texts critically and imaginatively,** select and evaluate textual detail to illustrate and support interpretations.
AO2	Explain how **language**, **structure** and **form** contribute to writers' presentation of ideas, themes and settings.
AO3	Make **comparisons and explain links** between texts, evaluating writers' different ways of expressing meaning and achieving effects.

Your **spelling, punctuation and grammar** will also be awarded marks.

Remember that **you'll be awarded marks for the quality of your response** rather than for the number of points you make. It's far better to make **critical, insightful comments** than to merely point out the poet's techniques.

Allocating Your Time

You should spend about 45 minutes on Section A. You could allocate your time as follows:
- **5–10 minutes** to **choose your question** and **make a plan**
- **30–35 minutes** to **write your answer**
- around **5 minutes** to **check your work** when you've finished.

Choosing Your Question

1 **Read both questions** for your cluster carefully.

2 **Highlight the key words** and think about how you would answer each question.

2 **Consider how much you know about the named poems and which poems** would offer the best comparison.

The table below suggests the main points of comparison between the poems in the cluster. It will help you identify poems to compare in the exam.

The crosses show the significant features of each poem so it's easy to see where the similarities and differences are.

		Flag	Extract from Out of the Blue	Mametz Wood	The Yellow Palm	The Right Word	At the Border, 1979	Belfast Confetti	Poppies	Futility	The Charge of the Light Brigade	Bayonet Charge	The Falling Leaves	'Come on, Come back'	next to of course god america i	Hawk Roosting
Themes / Key ideas	Reality of conflict		x	x	x	x		x		x	x	x		x		
	Patriotism	x					x				x	x			x	
	Conflict affecting the individual		x		x		x	x	x	x		x		x		
	Symbols of conflict	x			x	x	x		x						x	
	Anti-war	x			x	x				x				x	x	
	Memory			x			x				x	x		x		
	Grief		x						x				x			
	Women and conflict					x			x				x	x		
	Power			x											x	x
Form / structure	Free verse			x						x				x	x	
	Change in tone				x							x			x	
	First person		x		x	x	x	x	x			x				x
Language	Personification			x							x	x			x	x
	Use of contrasts	x			x	x	x									
	Contemplative			x	x	x				x		x	x			
	Irony	x					x	x						x	x	
	Repetition	x			x	x						x		x		
	Oxymoron													x	x	
	Onomatopoeia											x				
	Appeal to senses		x	x			x	x	x		x	x	x	x		x

Only the most obvious points of comparison are shown on this table. Use your knowledge of the poems to find unique features to create a personal response.

Planning Your Answer

How to Plan

Having a clear plan will help you to write a structured response and gives you something to refer back to if you get stuck while writing.

Your plan should be **brief and easy to read.**

In your plan, make notes about the following aspects of both poems:
- ideas about **conflict**
- the **key ideas** or **themes**
- how the poem is **structured**
- the **language** used in the poem.

There's no need to go into a lot of detail or to write in full sentences when planning. Use **key words and phrases** that will jog your memory when you look back at the plan. Make a note of the line references of quotations you could use to support your answer. If the quotations are very short, you could write down the whole thing.

Structure your plan in any way you want. You could use a **bullet-pointed list, table, mind map** or any other format that you're comfortable with.

As the time available in the exam is extremely limited, don't spend lots of time planning or writing an introduction or conclusion. An introductory sentence stating which poems you'll be comparing is enough.

Here are some example plans for a question comparing how ideas about conflict are presented in *The Charge of the Light Brigade* and *Mametz Wood*.

Bullet-Pointed List

Ideas about conflict 'The Charge of the Light Brigade' and 'Mametz Wood'.

Idea about conflict
- *(CLB) Admiration for the soldiers and their actions Shock at what happened to them*
- *(MW) Horror at what happened Sadness*

Theme
- *(CLB) Patriotism – it is right to fight and to die for your country – 'noble six hundred' Feeling that they were betrayed by the people who should have looked out for them The reality of war – not everyone can survive – 'not the six hundred'*
- *(MW) The reality of war – soldiers cut down in their prime, 'boots that outlasted them' Lasting impact of war*

Structure
- *(CLB) Final stanza is shorter than the others – suggests that their lives were cut off too soon? Rhythm reflects sound of the battle*
- *(MW) Chronological – suggests that the impact of war is long-lasting*

Language
- *(CLB) Pride – 'noble' Semantic field of death 'Death', 'hell', 'shatter'd and sunder'd' Violent*
- *(MW) Semantic field of negativity 'wasted young', 'a wound', 'dance-macabre' Personification*

Table

	'The Charge of the Light Brigade'	'Mametz Wood'
Idea about conflict	Admiration for the soldiers and their actions Shock at what happened to them	Horror at what happened Sadness
Theme	Patriotism – it is right to fight and to die for your country – 'noble six hundred' Feeling that they were betrayed by the people who should have looked out for them The reality of war – not everyone can survive – 'not the six hundred'	The reality of war – soldiers cut down in their prime, 'boots that outlasted them' Lasting impact of war
Structure	Final stanza is shorter than the others – suggests that their lives were cut off too soon? Rhythm reflects sound of the battle	Chronological – suggests that the impact of war is long-lasting
Language	Pride – 'noble' Semantic field of death 'Death', 'hell', 'shatter'd and sunder'd' Violent	Semantic field of negativity 'wasted young', 'a wound', 'dance-macabre' Personification

Mind Map

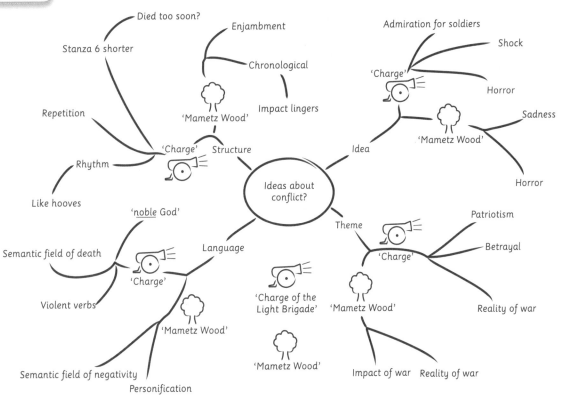

Writing a Comparative Essay

Finding Similarities and Differences

In your response to the question, you need to explain how the two poems are **similar** and how they are **different**, and **give examples** to back up your points.

As part of your revision, you could use a table like the one below to identify these similarities and differences. In each line make a brief note of the main points. Focus on identifying **interesting points of comparison** that you can explore in detail in the exam.

	Titles of poems go here	
	Similarities	**Differences**
Conflict		
Character		
Voice / viewpoint		
Themes		
Form		
Structure		
Language		
Tone		
My response		

Discourse Markers

Discourse markers are the glue that holds your answer together. They show the examiner the relationship between your ideas and arguments. Some examples of discourse markers that you could use are given below.

To show comparison	Although	Conversely	Despite
	Equally	However	In contrast
	Similarly	Whereas	While

To add information	Furthermore	In addition	In fact
	Moreover	By the same token	In connection with this

To introduce an example	For example	For instance	Specifically
	This illustrates	This is demonstrated	In relation to this

Writing a Comparative Essay

Using Quotations

You'll need to select **quotations** from the poems to support the points you make. Choose your quotations carefully, keep them short and make sure they relate to the point you're making.

Always **aim to write as much as you can about each piece of quoted text**; there should be more of your words on the answer paper than the poet's.

For each quotation think about:

- **the techniques** the writer has used
- **what** this technique contributes to our understanding of the poem
- **why** the writer may have used this technique, i.e. the writer's purpose.

Shaping Your Paragraphs

The following example outlines a format that you could use to structure a comparative paragraph, looking at how different features are used in each poem. This approach will help to make your comparative points very clear.

Begins with a topic sentence.	Both 'The Charge of the Light Brigade' and 'Mametz Wood' are poems about real conflicts. The first is about a battle in the Crimean war, and the second is about the aftermath of the First World War. In the first poem, Tennyson uses the rhythm of the poem to suggest the movement of the horses as they go into battle: 'half a league, half a league, / half a league onward' which makes the reader feel as though we are there watching the action. This makes it all the more shocking when we discover how the battle ends. In the second poem, the poet shocks us in a different way; by describing the 'socketed heads tilted back at an angle'. This is a gruesome image which brings to life the horror of this conflict.
Acknowledges that there is a difference between them.	
Refers to detail from the first poem.	
Gives a quotation from the first poem.	
Develops point more fully.	
Makes a clear link between poems which draws attention to the similarities and differences.	
Gives a quotation from the second poem.	
Develops point more fully.	

Tips for Writing a Comparative Essay

- Make sure you understand what you're comparing – note the key words in the question.
- Try to write a **balanced** response: don't favour one poem over the other.
- Structure your answer by taking one aspect (e.g. imagery) and exploring it in both poems.
- Start a new paragraph for each aspect you compare.
- Use **discourse markers** to signal the relationship between your ideas.
- If two aspects are significantly different, don't shy away. Highlight the fact and explain why / what difference this makes to the way you respond to the poem.
- Ensure you **maintain the comparison** throughout your answer.
- Use **quotations** to support each point you make about the poems.

Worked Sample Questions

Foundation Tier

Compare the ways in which ideas about soldiers are presented in 'The Charge of the Light Brigade' and **one** other poem from 'Conflict'.

Remember to compare:
- the ideas about soldiers
- the methods that the writers use.

(36 marks)

Solid introduction setting out the poems for discussion.	In 'The Charge of the Light Brigade' the soldiers are presented as heroes who are fighting for their country. In 'The Right Word', soldiers are presented as normal people who other people judge because of the side that they are on.
It's fine to abbreviate a title like this.	'Charge' is a poem which presents soldiers as doing the right thing for their country. They follow the orders that they are given because it is 'theirs not to reason why' which shows that they do what they are told because it is their job. They are described as brave because they rode 'into the valley of Death'. This shows that they knew that they were likely to die but they did it anyway because they were fighting for their country.
Good use of a quotation to support a point, and some development of the idea.	
Good use of a quotation but could have been developed more fully.	
Where is the supporting evidence?	In 'The Right Word', people who are fighting for their country are called lots of different negative names. This suggests that people who fight for their country are often looked at by other people in a negative way because they are the enemy. The poem shows that people don't think about who the soldiers really are; they just see the uniform.
A good point – needs supporting evidence though.	
A good point with supporting evidence.	In this poem, the word 'shadow' is repeated which makes it sound like the soldiers are hiding themselves. This makes the reader feel that they are being cowardly compared to the soldiers in 'Charge' who are 'noble' and show themselves to the enemy with pride. The soldiers in 'Charge' are brave because they are described as riding into battle with 'Cannon to right of them / Cannon to left of them' which shows that they were outnumbered. In 'The Right Word' they hide in the shadows which makes the reader feel that they are not brave at all. This is surprising when you compare it to the other poem because you would expect all soldiers to be brave.
Makes a clear link between the poems for the first time.	
This point could have been developed more fully.	
Clear focus on the reader's response.	
Good point with supporting evidence. Could have developed the point by analysing 'child' fully.	The poet shows that people make judgements on other people by saying that the soldier at the door is actually a 'child'. This shows that soldiers are people like everyone else and that people should not be so judgemental about them. In 'Charge', soldiers are not presented as ordinary people at all: the poet thinks that they are true heroes for what they have done. As well as calling them 'noble', he calls them 'hero' and describes them riding 'boldly they rode and well' which shows that he thinks they are brave. This is different from the soldiers in the other poem.
A comparison is made but could have been developed further.	

40

In 'The Right Word' the poet shows that the soldiers are ordinary people when she says at the end of the poem that the soldier 'takes off his shoes' when he comes into the house. This shows that people were wrong when they judged him negatively because he is just a person like anyone else when you get to know him. This makes the reader feel that people should not be so judgemental because then they would understand people more. This links with the title of the poem.

In 'Charge' the poet makes it obvious that he does not think that soldiers are ordinary people at all when he calls them 'hero'. This shows that he thinks that what they did was something special which people should be proud of and makes the reader feel that they did something impressive and important. This is different to the other poem.

> A point about structure which could have been developed more fully.

> This is correct but it could have been developed more fully.

> A point about language which could have been developed.

> A comparison is made but could have been developed further.

Examiner's Comments

This is a C/D grade response. It is a sound answer which makes some connections between the poems. There are some supporting quotations and some reference to their impact on the reader. The candidate has made some points about language, although there is only one comment on structure, which is undeveloped. A short conclusion would help to draw all of the ideas together.

To achieve a C grade, this student should:
- Make sure that quotations are given in support of each point.
- Focus more closely on key words and phrases and their effects.
- Consider clearly the effect on the reader.
- Make closer reference to structure.
- Use more poetic terminology in support of the 'methods' part of the question.

Worked Sample Questions

Higher Tier

Compare how ideas about patriotism are presented in 'At the Border, 1979' and **one** other poem from 'Conflict'.

(36 marks)

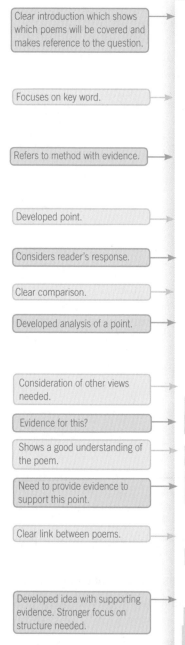

Clear introduction which shows which poems will be covered and makes reference to the question.

Focuses on key word.

Refers to method with evidence.

Developed point.

Considers reader's response.

Clear comparison.

Developed analysis of a point.

Consideration of other views needed.

Evidence for this?

Shows a good understanding of the poem.

Need to provide evidence to support this point.

Clear link between poems.

Developed idea with supporting evidence. Stronger focus on structure needed.

In 'At the Border, 1979', patriotism is clearly linked with a sense of place, as the poet describes her family's response to the border crossing. This is shown to be a positive thing through the language that is used. On the other hand 'Flag' suggests that patriotism can be something more dangerous than this.

In 'Border', the poet describes how her mother 'informed me: We are going home'. This shows that, for her mother, being 'home' is important, and that she sees 'home' not as the place she is, but the place she is from. The poet uses positive language such as 'cleaner' and 'kinder' which effectively shows her mother's patriotic belief that 'home' is better than anywhere else. When the adults tell them that 'soon everything will taste different' they are suggesting that one place is better than another. This is hyperbolic and shows how emotional people's response to 'home' is and how patriotism is not always rational. This makes the reader question whether this is a logical thing to feel.

In 'Flag' on the other hand, the poet sees patriotism as being something that can be dangerous. He looks at the flag which is 'just a piece of cloth' and sees it as a symbol of patriotism which 'brings a nation to its knees.' This is a negative image and suggests that patriotism is not always a good thing. When he writes that it 'makes the guts of men grow bold' this shows that people are made to feel braver and stronger by being patriotic, which the reader might think is a good thing. However, this can lead to war, which the poet does not seem to agree with.

In 'Border', the poet shows contrasting views of patriotism. The adults are all emotionally attached to their country, but the children see things differently because they notice that the land is the same on the other side of the border. This suggests that patriotism is something that is only important to adults and that children are more accepting of differences. This is similar to the idea in 'Flag' because the poet can see that it is 'just' a flag, but patriotic people see it as something more than that. This is similar to the idea in 'Border' that one place is better than another. At the end of 'Flag', the poet says that people who 'possess such a cloth' need to 'blind your conscience to the end' which shows that he thinks that patriotism is a bad thing because it can make people do things that they might not otherwise do.

At the end of 'Border' the poet says 'the same chain of mountains encompassed all of us' which shows that she thinks that people are all the same really because we are all part of the same world. This suggests that she thinks that she doesn't really understand why people are patriotic, because we are all really the same. This is shown when she says 'it rained on both sides of the chain' meaning that things are the same everywhere, no matter where you are from.

> Good points which could have been developed with closer analysis of key words as well as more developed focus on structure.

The tone of 'Flag' is very cynical and makes it clear that the poet thinks that unthinking patriotism is wrong because it causes harm. When he says that it 'will outlive the blood you bleed' this makes the reader feel that it is wrong that patriotism can cause people to die for 'just a piece of cloth'. Although 'Border' seems to challenge the idea of patriotism too, because both sides of the border are the same, I don't think it is as cynical as 'Flag'. I think the poet is saying that patriotism is a strange thing, because one place is like every other place, but I don't think she thinks it is a bad thing.

> Clear focus on detail with consideration of the reader's response and use of an embedded quotation.

> Clear personal response is given.

Overall, I think that both poems question the idea of patriotism but for different reasons. Hardi seems to think that patriotism is harmless but wonders why people are so patriotic, but Agard thinks that it is dangerous.

> Clear conclusion.

Examiner's Comments

This is an A grade response. It is a strong answer which focuses on detail in an analytical manner and makes very clear links between the poems.

The answer is well structured and gives consideration to language and structure, as well as making reference to the effectiveness of the writers' choices.

To achieve an A*, this student should:
- Consider a range of possible meanings for key phrases.
- Develop ideas about structure in more detail.
- Evaluate the effectiveness of the writer's methods, perhaps commenting on the titles of the poems.

Exam Practice Questions

Foundation Tier

1 Compare the ways in which writers explore conflict in 'Flag' and **one** other poem from 'Conflict'. Remember to compare:
- what they say about conflict
- the methods that the writers use.   *(36 marks)*

2 Compare the ways in which ideas about the reality of war are presented in 'The Charge of the Light Brigade' and **one** other poem from 'Conflict'. Remember to compare:
- what they say about the reality of war
- the methods that the writers use.   *(36 marks)*

3 Compare the ways in which the effects of war on the individual are presented in *'Extract from* Out of the Blue' and **one** other poem from 'Conflict'. Remember to compare:
- what they say about the effect of war on the individual
- the methods that the writers use.   *(36 marks)*

Higher Tier

1 Compare how ideas about patriotism are shown in 'At the Border, 1979' and **one** other poem from 'Conflict'.   *(36 marks)*

2 Compare how an anti-war message is presented in 'Futility' and **one** other poem from 'Conflict'.   *(36 marks)*

3 Compare how symbols of conflict are presented in 'Poppies' and **one** other poem from 'Conflict'.   *(36 marks)*

Answers

These answers are only intended as a starting point and suggest 'obvious' comparisons. The tables show the main points of comparison; try to come up with some of your own ideas too, then pick four or five points of comparison and refer to the poems and find examples to analyse in detail.

Foundation Tier

1.   You might compare *Flag* with *Belfast Confetti* or *The Falling Leaves*

Flag	The flag inspires conflict because it is a symbol of patriotism. The poem explores the consequences of unthinkingly following the flag through use of the dismissive 'just', and shows the poet's cynical view of people's actions.
Belfast Confetti	Vivid description of being caught up in conflict. Ellipsis and onomatopoeia suggest the sounds of the conflict. Accumulation used to create a sense of fear. Conflict close to home.
The Falling Leaves	An extended metaphor for dying soldiers. 'gallant multitude' suggests bravery and also the number of soldiers dying. Positive language shows bravery of soldiers. Negative language reflects attitude to conflict.

2.   You might compare *The Charge of the Light Brigade* with *Mametz Wood* or *Bayonet Charge*

The Charge of the Light Brigade	A vivid description of the battle. Use of verbs and the rhythm of the poem convey the sights and sounds of the battle. The accumulation of the lines about 'cannon to left of them…' shows how dangerous their situation was and explains why 'not the six hundred' came back.
Mametz Wood	Describes the aftermath of the war and how skeletons are unearthed years later. The description of the skeletons with 'their socketed heads tilted back at an angle' is shocking and the image of the 'wound' is a reminder of the lasting effects of conflict.
Bayonet Charge	Describes war as it happens. Violent verbs and enjambment help to emphasise the panic as the soldier runs for cover. The shocking image of the hare reflects the idea that war is terrible, and the dismissive 'etcetera' shows the idea that patriotism is meaningless in the face of battle.

Exam Practice Questions

3. You might compare *Extract from Out of the Blue* with 'Come on, Come Back' or *The Yellow Palm*

Extract from Out of the Blue	First person emphasises the effect of conflict on the individual, although the reference to 'others like me' shows that conflict has a greater impact than that. The reader is an observer – as was the speaker until this event, which shows the broad impact of conflict. Shows the 'appalling' impact of conflict.
'Come on, Come Back'	Juxtaposition of the effect on the individual with the unemotional language of 'human exterminators'. Shows the confusion and fear caused by conflict, and the consequences. The 'enemy sentinel' is a reminder that conflict makes strangers of people who are essentially the same.
The Yellow Palm	Shocking images of 'blood on the walls' describes daily life for people caught in conflict. Focus is on the impact on civilians rather than on soldiers. Juxtaposes symbols of peace, 'lilac stems', with threat, 'a Cruise missile'.

Higher Tier

1. You might compare *At the Border, 1979* with *next to of course god america i* or *The Charge of the Light Brigade*

At the Border, 1979	Patriotism is linked to place: the significance of the word 'home'. Suggests that an adult's view of place and a child's are different – the adult response is emotional whilst the child's is not.
next to of course god america i	Suggests that patriotism is integral to American life but that being patriotic is not necessarily a good thing. Simile shows courage and determination. Oxymoron of 'these heroic happy dead' shows that unthinking patriotism has negative consequences.
The Charge of the Light Brigade	Repetition of 'Theirs not to' shows unquestioning action and celebrates patriotism: 'noble six hundred'. The poem has a clear semantic field of pride in their achievements.

2. You might compare *Futility* with 'Come on, Come Back' or *The Right Word*

Futility	Focus on the death of one soldier and the 'futility' of war. Use of emotive language to show his feeling. Sonnet form shows his love for the soldiers. Questions in final stanza suggest that the poet is challenging the idea of conflict.
'Come on, Come Back'	The aftermath of war is as important as the war itself: she has been reduced to 'a child, an idiot, [...] one without memory'. Shocking imagery shows impact of war. Irony of connection with the 'enemy' questions the purpose of war.
The Right Word	People create conflict from the words that they use. It uses pejorative language to show people's negative perceptions and references to shadows to suggest that conflict is also caused by lack of understanding. Suggests that choosing the 'right word' could reduce conflict.

3. You might compare *Poppies* with *Flag* or *At the Border, 1979*

Poppies	A symbol of the fallen. Dove is a symbol of peace. Everyday imagery as a reminder that the 'individual war graves' contain ordinary people. Contemplative tone. Symbols are for those left behind.
Flag	Although 'just a piece of cloth', the flag is a symbol of patriotism and used to 'bring a nation to its knees' – dismissive language used to reduce the symbol's power. Belief in the symbol has far reaching consequences.
At the Border, 1979	The 'thick iron chain' is a symbol of separation. Shows that conflict is man-made. Children see beyond the symbol but adults can't. Semantic fields of difference and similarity are used to show different attitudes.

Quick Test Answers

Example answers have been provided for the quick tests however they are intended as guidance only; wherever possible try to think of other comments and examples you could give in response to the questions.

Pages 4–5

1. It inspires them to do things that they might not otherwise do. It can motivate people, make brave men out of cowards and control countries.

2. He writes about 'a' flag to show that this could happen anywhere in the world. He says that it is 'just a piece of cloth' suggesting that it is really nothing special but that people allow it to have power over them. He uses emotive language to suggest that there are many negative associations that can be made with the flag.

3. No. He is being sarcastic. He would not be friends with people who do not think about the consequences of their beliefs and actions. This is also being used to show that people sometimes use the word to suggest a relationship that isn't real in an attempt to make people think in the same way as the person who says it.

4. He thinks that they have not thought about the consequences of what they do, and their consciences must be blind.

Pages 6–7

1. The speaker is described as having a 'white cotton shirt' which suggests that he is a civilian. He writes about 'others like me' which links all of the victims together. The references in lines 11 and 12 link him to ordinary people doing ordinary things.

2. The poem is in the first person which makes it feel real. To begin with, the speaker is hopeful of escape because he writes that 'you have noticed now' which suggests that he thinks that he can be saved. In line 9, he still seems to have hope that someone will come and save him. By the end of the poem, he has given up hope and the image of his 'sagging' arm suggests that he can't go on any longer. He also knows that he has to jump if he is going to prevent himself from burning to death – but this seems like a terrible choice to have to make. The verbs describing the falling victims are horrific images because we know that there is no hope for them.

3. There are constant references to 'seeing' and the reader knows that this event was seen on television all over the world. The poem is in chronological order and shows what people would have seen: the shock at the start and then the people falling from the towers, so it seems very realistic.

Pages 8–9

1. Lots of the words in the poem suggest that he thinks that conflict is a waste of lives. He calls them 'the wasted young' and suggests that they were young and fragile. He doesn't think that they deserved to die. The fact that he writes the poem about them suggests that he wants to make sure that they are not forgotten.

2. In stanza 3, 'they were told to walk, not run' which makes them seem as though they were treated like children. The idea that the skeletons were 'linked arm in arm' also makes them sound like children, holding onto each other for comfort and protection. The men have rotted away to 'socketed heads' but their 'boots [...] outlasted them' which makes it sound like they were very young.

3. He suggests that people forget things that have happened in the past until something happens to make them remember, like the finding of the bodies in the grave. This suggests that people are not really bothered about things that don't directly affect them.

Pages 10–11

1. That their lives are unsettled. There is lots of vibrant life and colour in the poem which suggests that they have positive things in their lives, but he also describes violent and negative things such as blood in the mosque. There is a sense that they are always waiting for the next attack because he describes the Cruise missile almost as if it's an ordinary thing to see.

2. He writes about it in an unemotional way which suggests that he feels detached from it. He sees shocking and violent scenes which he describes using negative language but he also sees the beauty in the place, which suggests that he is able to see beyond conflict.

3. Any suitable response, for example: I think he is undecided about where the conflict will end because the end of the poem is ambiguous. It could be hopeful because it ends with the yellow palms and salaams, but it also refers to the fruit dropping which could suggest that people will go on dying.

Pages 12–13

1. She thinks that a lack of understanding of other people can be a cause of conflict. She also thinks that the language that we use can either cause conflict or make it worse.

2. She says that she is looking for the 'right word' – one that doesn't cause conflict. She uses emotive and pejorative language to show the negative effects that it can have on people and situations and challenges the reader through her use of pronouns to think again about the language that they use.

3. She thinks that if people can find 'the right word' that will help to alleviate conflict. At the end of the poem, the fact that the person is a child suggests that if people can see past language to people, then conflict might be avoidable.

Pages 14–15

1. The adults see the border as the space between where they are and 'home'. They have an emotional response to it because it is keeping them from a place where they think that everything is better. The children see the border as something insignificant, and treat the border crossing as a bit of a game.

2. She uses emotive language like 'home' and says that 'mothers were crying' to show their emotional response. She uses hyperbole to show how strongly the people feel about the border. On the other hand, the semantic field of similarity is linked with the children who simply see that the land is the same 'both sides of the chain'.

3. They show that conflict can come from lack of understanding. In the poem, both sides of the border are actually the same, physically, but people view them differently. It isn't the places themselves that are a source of conflict; it is the attitudes towards them.

Pages 16–17

1. He feels frightened by it. It is a dangerous and dramatic thing to be part of.

2. He uses onomatopoeia and ellipsis to suggest the sounds of the conflict, and uses accumulation to list all of the effects of the bomb. The use of jargon makes the reader feel disconcerted because they don't understand: just like they would feel if this happened to them.

3. No. Although it is about an incident in Ireland, the reference to other battles suggests that he is writing about conflict in general.

Pages 18–19

1. She seems to feel sad about conflict. There is a sense of regret in the poem as she watches her son leave, but she doesn't try to stop him. This suggests that she accepts the idea of conflict – although she doesn't want her child to be part of it. When she says 'all my words flattened' it is as if she has stopped trying to change his mind: he is 'intoxicated' by the idea of becoming a soldier. At the end of the poem, she suggests that for some people, conflict will be the end of their relationships because their sons will never come back.

2. That it is traumatic. Without their loved ones, those left behind are always 'hoping to hear' and waiting nervously for them to come back, or for news of them.

3. The songbird represents her son. It leaves, like he does, looking for freedom. The dove is a symbol of peace, which might suggest that she is hoping for peace. It can also be a symbol of mourning.

Pages 20–21

1. At first it seems that he is talking about trying to wake the dead being futile, but it's actually about conflict itself. He thinks that life is futile if we waste it by going to war and dying young. He also seems to suggest that religious belief might be futile, since nothing could save the soldier.

2. From the start of the poem, he uses negative language to show that it is 'futile' to try to wake the soldier. He talks about the past and the present, and about warmth and cold, which shows the contrast between life and death. The fact that he refers to the dead soldier as 'still warm' is shocking and shows how pointless war is. At the end of the poem, the question makes the reader ask the same question as the poet, and come to the same conclusion: that war is futile.

3. Any suitable response, for example: I think it is more effective. People know that the act of war is bloody and terrible, but this poem focuses more on the emotional side and the personal loss, which makes it more real and shocking.

Pages 22–23

1. Firstly, he writes a poem about them, which suggests that he feels that their achievement should be celebrated. He uses words such as 'noble' and 'hero' which are clearly positive. He also reflects on the fact that they were patriotic, which is something that was considered very important at the time.

2. He uses onomatopoeia and rhythm to suggest the sounds of the battle, which seems terrifying. He repeats 'cannon' to show that they were surrounded and personifies the place that were in, as well as calling it 'Hell'. When he writes that 'not the six hundred' came back, that shows that they gave their lives for their country.

3. It suggests that the soldiers' lives were cut short, but it also seems like an epitaph to them – something which people will remember them by. It uses positive language such as 'honour' and 'glory' which makes it clear that he thinks that they should be remembered forever as heroes.

Pages 24–25

1. The poem opens in the middle of the battle. The use of verbs shows that he is moving fast to avoid being killed. There is onomatopoeia and description of the way he 'lugged' his gun to show how he is struggling to get away from danger. The shocking image of the hare shows that nothing is safe.

2. He thinks that it is terrifying and that people who are involved in war are simply doing as they are told without thinking. When they think about what they are doing, they are terrified too.

3. Through images of fear and death. He also thinks that people give good reasons for going to war like 'king, honour, human dignity' but that when they're in a war, nothing matters but surviving.

Pages 26–27

1. That it is a waste of lives. She describes how the soldiers die too soon.

2. She says they are 'slain by no wind of age' and she talks about their 'beauty'. She thinks that soldiers are 'gallant' but that too many of them die. She links them to the leaves which fall 'thickly, silently' which means that they die in great numbers without saying anything. This might mean that they die patriotically, but that she doesn't think that is a good reason to die.

3. Leaves fall all the time without people really thinking about them. This suggests that she thinks the same is true of the soldiers: people don't notice or really care about their deaths.

4. They are something beautiful which only last a short time before vanishing forever. She thinks that the dead soldiers are like that, and will soon be forgotten.

Pages 28–29

1. She describes the conflict in quite an unemotional way which makes it seem more shocking. She used words like 'exterminator' to show how brutal conflict is. The fact that the persona in the poem is alive but commits suicide suggests that conflict has long lasting repercussions which some people never recover from.

2. She suggests that an enemy is just another person, and that they might actually have more in common with you than you think.

3. She suggests that it is inevitable, and that all war has a profound impact on the people involved.

Pages 30–31

1. He makes intertextual references to two famous American songs, which every American is likely to know. He personifies America which suggests that people think of it not just as a place but a thing to be respected.

2. He questions the clichés that people use to suggest that people think in clichés and therefore don't question what they are being asked to do. He uses dismissive language to show his view that patriotism is unthinking. He uses emotive words like 'slaughter' to show that unquestioning patriotism can lead to violent death. At the end of the poem, the 'drank rapidly' might suggest that the speaker is afraid of speaking out, because challenging patriotism is a risky thing to do.

3. Any suitable response, for example: I think it is a love poem for people who give their lives in the name of their country. Although it is clearly linked to America, I think it could be about anyone.

Pages 32–33

1. The poet uses personal pronouns such as 'I' and 'mine' to show that the hawk thinks that it is the centre of the universe. The references to 'Creation' suggest that the hawk believes that the world was created for it to use, and that it thinks it has more power than God.

2. In stanza 3, the poet refers to killing 'because it is all mine' which might refer to leaders who take over lands that they want. In line 20, the idea that the hawk doesn't have to justify its actions also links to this idea.

3. He says 'nothing has changed since I began' but this is not true, because he also refers to the sun, which moves. This suggests that the hawk's arrogance might lead it to make mistakes, and that it can't achieve what it sets out to do in the last line.

Glossary of Key Words

Accumulation – listing of ideas which builds up to create a particular effect.

Alliteration – repetition of a sound at the beginning of words.

Ambiguous – unclear in meaning (ambiguity).

Caesura – a pause in a line of poetry. Usually in the middle of a line but sometimes at the start of (initial) or the end (terminal).

Chronological – in time order from beginning to end.

Cliché – an overused expression.

Colloquial – informal language often used in conversation.

Consonance – repetition of similar consonant sounds.

Contemplative – thoughtful.

Cyclical – begins and ends at the same time or place.

Direct speech – the exact words someone has said, in quotation marks.

Dramatic monologue – a poem in the voice of one person, which is not the poet. The content of the poem reveals the nature of the speaker's character.

Elegy – a poem of mourning. May also refer to a poem that reflects on death and passing time in a melancholy mood (elegiac).

Ellipsis – trailing dots (…) which are used to suggest a pause for thought.

Emotive – appealing to the emotions / evoking strong feelings.

End-stopped – a line in a poem which ends with a piece of punctuation rather than running into the next line.

Enjambment – when a clause or sentence runs from one line of poetry to another, undisturbed by punctuation.

Euphemism – the use of a word which has a harmless meaning instead of one which is more direct or controversial.

Extended metaphor – a metaphor which is developed over a longer period, for example a whole poem.

First person – a narrative viewpoint where the narrator is involved and refers to 'I' or 'me'.

Foreground – making one idea stand out as being more important than others.

Half-rhyme – rhyme where the consonant sounds are similar but the vowel sounds are not.

Hyperbole – exaggeration.

Imagery – a collection of devices (including metaphors, similes, personification and synecdoche) which use language to create vivid visual descriptions.

Imperative – an instruction or command, such as 'sit' or 'run'.

Interjection – an interruption which expresses emotion.

Intertextual references – references made by an author to other literary texts.

Irony – the tension created through the opposition of a literal meaning and an underlying meaning.

Jargon – technical language drawn from a particular field of knowledge or expertise, e.g. medicine, the law, business.

Juxtaposition – the placing of (often contrasting) words or phrases next to each other.

Lament – a poem which expresses grief and mourning.

Metaphor – a form of imagery where one thing is said to be another, suggesting similarities between the two.

Onomatopoeia – a word which is written to suggest a sound, e.g. 'crash'.

Oxymoron – the use of words which have contrasting meanings in order to emphasise one meaning, e.g. 'a deafening silence'.

Paradox – something which appears to contradict itself.

Parody – a text which mocks another text by imitation.

Pejorative language – deliberately negative language.

Personification – a form of imagery that gives animals, ideas or inanimate objects human qualities.

Present tense – the form of a verb describing an action happening at the present time.

Pronoun – a word such as 'I' or 'he' which can be substituted for a person's name.

Rhyme – repetition of sounds.

Rhythm – the beat of the writing – fast or slow, regular or irregular.

Semantic field – a group of words which have a common theme or meaning.

Simile – a comparison using the words 'like' or 'as'.

Sonnet – a love poem which is 14 lines in length.

Stanza – a group of lines in a poem that may have a shared meaning, metre or rhyme scheme.

Third person – when a text is written about 'he', 'she' or 'it', it is in the third person.

Verb – a word that describes an action or state.